Sheba's Quest

*To my lovely grandchildren, with the prayer that
like Sheba they too will ask a man of God
'hard questions'about the Lord, resulting in
eternal 'satisfaction'.*

Sheba's Quest

Peter Trumper

BELFAST, NORTHERN IRELAND
GREENVILLE, SOUTH CAROLINA

ISBN 1 84030 146 5

Published by the Ambassador Group
Ambassador Publications
a division of
Ambassador Productions Ltd.
Providence House
Ardenlee Street,
Belfast,
BT6 8QJ
Northern Ireland
www.ambassador-productions.com
&
Ambassador Emerald International
427 Wade Hampton Blvd.
Greenville
SC 29609, USA
www.emeraldhouse.com

Introduction

The Queen of Sheba is undoubtedly one of history's most fascinating personalities, the subject of stories both biblical and romantic; the lady who courageously traversed an arid desert for over 1,200 miles to meet King Solomon.

For 3,000 years their names have been linked together, the phrase 'Solomon and Sheba' being as familiar to most people as 'knife and fork'; reference was even made to them by Christ himself (Matt. 12:42). Yet, despite her fame, how little is known about her and the reason behind her momentous visit to Jerusalem! Some say she arrived from Egypt on a trade mission, had a romantic affair with Solomon, and left Israel pregnant with his child. From such stories dreams and Hollywood movies arise!

IN SEARCH OF TRUTH

In fact, as this book relates, it was not commerce that caused Sheba to journey such a distance (as Queen she would have appointed a delegation to see to that), but rather the irresistible grace of the living God. Her heart ached, not for trading agreements or romance but for truth, and she was prepared to travel far to find it.

At the time, it was known throughout 'all nations round about' that far away in Jerusalem Israel's God had imparted a unique and astonishing wisdom to the nation's king. People flocked from near and far to hear it, even 'all kings' (1 Kings 4:31,34). Sheba joined the procession, despite the fact she was sceptical when she started out on her journey, as she later admitted (1 Kings 10:6-9).

However, after spending time 'communing' with Solomon and plying him with 'hard questions' (1 Kings 10:1,2), far from being disappointed, it was very much more than wisdom Sheba heard remarkable though it was, and something more astonishing than she could have imagined.

THE QUESTION OF THE QUESTIONS

But what were those 'hard questions' Sheba asked her royal host, and as the text does not tell us, have we a right to enquire? I suggest the text is silent, not to forbid an enquiry, but on the contrary to encourage one among those who delight in God's precious Word! After all, Sheba's quest concerned 'the name of the Lord' (1 Kings 10:1), and therefore Solomon's answers would have led her to that name. Their journey then is fascinating to chart, the direction they took all too obvious, and in this book I seek to follow it.

MORIAH

Only one name appears on the signpost: **'MORIAH',** and it directs us to three historic moments all of which undoubtedly featured in Sheba's quest. In chronological order, and the train of thought followed in this book: Isaac being prepared for sacrifice (Gen.22), the purchasing of Araunah's threshing floor (2 Sam.24), and the building of the temple (1 Kings 6-8).

In reverse order: the first question was waiting to be asked each day of Sheba's stay in Jerusalem, because a newly built and magnificent temple loomed large over the entire city (1 Kings 8), if not the nation: 'the house of the Lord at Jerusalem in mount **Moriah.** (2 Chron.3 :1)' No visitor could have resisted asking questions about it, and Solomon who had been instrumental in its erection would have been only too pleased to impart the necessary information.

That being so it must have included the subjects of God's holiness, the sinfulness of man, and therefore the reason for the priesthood and blood-sacrifice. In turn, somebody from Sheba's cultural background would need to be told how Solomon knew his God was holy, and besides, what are 'holiness' and 'sin'? The enquiry would automatically have led to Sinai: God's fiery manifestation on the Mount, the revelation of his character, and the tablets of stone upon which the Law was written (Exod.19-20; 32-34).

All that having been explained, it was a short step to asking why the temple was built on mount **Moriah?** If Sheba had failed to do so, Solomon would not have hesitated in telling her because it concerned his father David, to whom in any case one of the most remarkable of all prophecies had been revealed (2 Sam.7:16).

The location was chosen by God, and for a special reason: 'where the Lord appeared unto David. (2 Chron.3:1)' Then would have followed the account of that moment in David's life during a period of national crisis when he met the avenging angel 'by the threshing place of Araunah the Jebusite' on mount **Moriah,** pleading with him to spare the people of Jerusalem, and then when the request was granted erecting an altar on the spot in thanksgiving (2 Sam. 24:16, 17,24).

But the mount was very special for another reason, and could Solomon have resisted telling Sheba about it, particularly after establishing the fact that he and his guest were distantly related? As I reveal in this book, their lineage could be traced back to Abraham, the mighty Patriarch who was commanded by God to sacrifice his 'only son' Isaac: 'get thee into the land of **Moriah'** (Gen.22:2). There, in the area where the temple stood many years later, Isaac lay upon an altar with his father's knife hovering over him. Only a substituted ram saved Isaac's life. It was an extremely dramatic incident, but one pregnant with Gospel truth.

THE DESTINATION REACHED

With sanctified intelligence then it is possible to unravel the 'hard questions' that Sheba asked Solomon; to follow her train of thought, during that historic meeting between the two.

In turn, as the quest concerned 'the name of the Lord' a quickened soul will understand what was taking place between the two. The world refers to commerce or romance, but in fact, within his realm of Old Testament limitations Solomon was pointing Sheba to the 'name which is above every name', before whom 'every knee should bow. (Phil.2: 9,10)'

ONE
From the Land of Spices

She arrived at the gates of Jerusalem, having emerged from the shimmering haze of a desert heat – the sand burning under a scorching sun – accompanied by all the royal trappings of wealth and privilege befitting a queen.

The city's official recorder (1 Kings 4:3), who had served King David years earlier in the same capacity (2 Sam.8:16), could have told many stories relating to Jerusalem's comparatively brief history at that time, but the visit of the Queen of the South was something special (2 Sam.5:7). Even centuries later, the archives bulging with the details of remarkable events Jerusalem experienced over the many years, memories of the occasion had still not lost their appeal (1 Kings 10:1-13).

However, the recorder – Jehoshaphat by name (1 Kings 4:3), but not to be confused with the Judean king sixty years later – made no mention of how Jerusalem's citizens reacted to the visit that momentous day. Suddenly into the city had arrived, evidently from afar, the pomp and grandeur associated with monarchy: the regal splendour, the colourful display, the enviable opulence. What excitement must have swept through the city, stimulated by the crowds' curiosity, as they jostled for the finest vantage point to watch the Queen and her entourage passing by.

The vanguard, of what the recorder reported was 'a very great' procession (1 Kings 10:2), would have comprised an impressive array of 'valiant men' (Cant.3:7,8), weaponry glinting in the sunshine, to protect their sovereign and her treasures. Then into view, the excitement of the spectators increasing to an awe-inspired crescendo, appeared the jewel of the crown herself. She reclined upon a resplendent palanquin, suitably majestic and untouchable, carried aloft by powerfully muscular black arms. Following behind was a seemingly endless line of camels, whose ambling gait dictated the procession's dignified pace, heavily-laden with ornate chests containing the choicest of customary gifts as from one monarch to another: spices, precious stones and gold (1 Kings 10:2).

But the visitors, not least the Queen herself, had no interest in those who watched them open-mouthed. Their sole concern was for what lay ahead of them, and the reason for their exhausting journey to meet King Solomon (972-932BC) seated enthroned in 'glory' (Matt.6:29).

SWEET PERFUME OF MARVELLOUS SPICES

How long it had taken to reach Jerusalem is unknown, four months from Babylon in the east (Ezra 7:8), but incredibly the Queen and her travelling companions had journeyed as many as 1,250 miles across the arid Arabian desert. That is, from Arabia's deep south in what today is called the Yemen, and situated at the junction between the Red Sea and the Gulf of Aden. Not surprisingly, the ancient world considered the area 'the uttermost parts of the earth' (Matt.12:42).

There lay the seemingly idyllic beauty of Marib (Mareb) the capital city of the Kingdom of Sheba, where 'its inhabitants have great flocks of sheep in the meadows, and birds fly in from distant isles bringing leaves of pure cinnamon'. One could 'always smell the sweet perfume of marvellous spices, whether it be incense or wonderful myrrh', as Dionysius the Greek described the area in 90AD. From such descriptions legends are born.

TRADING PARTNERS

Geographically obscure it may have been to the citizens of Israel, but the Kingdom of Sheba was by no means unknown to their King and his courtiers, far from it. Solomon and the Queen of the South may never have met, but they were well known to each other through the trading process. His merchants penetrated Arabia with their richly laden caravans, while at the same time, his ships heavy with merchandise sailed the Red Sea heading for Arabian ports (1 Kings 9:26).

As for the Queen: her kingdom, the aptly named 'land of spices', was the greatest exporter of them in the ancient world (Ezek.27:22), travelling the 'incense road' (Jer.6:20) – together with gold, ivory and precious stones (Is.60:6) – towards Israel and beyond. (1 Kings 10:10) However, there was the slightest of sensitivities. The caravan trade route to Egypt, Phoenicia and Syria passed directly through Israel, it was therefore always expedient for Sheba's kingdom to be on friendly terms with the monarch of that strategically placed country.

FOR WHAT REASON?

Jerusalem's inquisitive citizens surely asked many questions that day, but apart from being surprised at her sudden appearance in their city, were they sufficiently sophisticated to enquire as to the reason behind the Queen's visit? Probably they assumed it was about trade. There is no doubt though their King and his courtiers knew there were questions to ask, not least, the most obvious one of all. The Kingdom of Sheba in the person of its Queen was most welcome, but why had it arrived? Surely, it could not only have been about commerce.

To begin with, this was not an ordinary state visit. The official recorder was unaware of the Queen having been formally invited, or informally for that matter; no courteous exchanges between the two monarchs and their ambassadors, as one would have expected on such an important occasion. Perhaps her desire to visit Jerusalem had whispered its way along the 'incense road', and had been heard by those most important people, the King's merchants who reported what they had heard to the palace. If that was so, the recorder does not appear to have been cognizant of the matter. In fact, to all intents and purposes, she just materialised in a swirl of sand!

Merchants, and their camel trains heaped high with merchandise, were commonplace in Jerusalem arriving and departing on a daily basis, but the King's officials recognised royalty when they saw it, even from a distance. That being so, the unexpected appearance of 'a very great company' approaching through the haze must have caused consternation among those concerned with hospitality arrangements (2 Chron.9: 1).

Despite the enormous size of the palace, and the extensive facilities, there would still have been much to arrange, and at short notice: accommodation for the Queen, her ladies-in-waiting, as well as her many retainers and guards. Then, of course, there were numerous camels and horses to attend to, to be unloaded, fed, watered and housed. One can easily imagine the palace being a hive of scurrying officials and servants that day, the more so, the nearer the caravan trundled its way towards the city gates.

However, once the initial shock had passed and there was time once again to ponder, other questions would have floated into view. For example, the Kingdom of Sheba having entered Jerusalem uninvited, why was the Monarch representing it? Why was not a delegation sent on the Queen's behalf? Monarchs invariably led their armies into battle (1 Kings 22:30), but it was not usual for them to lead missions for peace. That task was left to others (Luke 14:32). So, why had the Queen of Sheba arrived in person?

But the most extraordinary detail of all was the distance covered in order to reach Jerusalem. A round trip of 2,500 miles through rough terrain and blistering heat was a journey a Bedouin warrior might have hesitated to make – but a woman, and one accustomed to wearing 'soft clothing' (Matt.11:8)? Clearly, the Queen was more-than-extremely anxious to visit the city, which would appear to argue against one concerned only with economy.

In earlier times, the humble donkey was the main means of desert transport, making its lowly way from watering hole to watering hole. This meant the traveller was confined to a set route, and therefore in greater danger from marauding bands, who knew their victims' whereabouts and of their vulnerability too. At a later date, though, the lumbering camel was broken in and harnessed. These 'ships of the desert' could carry many more burdens than a donkey, and did not require as much water, which provided travellers with access to fresh routes. But still, despite this, and the fact that the Queen had spent her life in a desert environment – 2,500 miles, just to discuss trade? It seems unlikely; that more, much more, was involved.

THOUGHTS FROM AFAR

The recorder knew the actual reasons for the undoubted risks the Queen took in journeying so far from the security of Marib, that she might meet a foreign monarch whose country was so different from her own. It was because of Solomon's fame, which was widespread, intriguingly so (2 Chron.9:1).

But then, the Queen was famous among her contemporaries too, as were numerous other national leaders. However, unlike them, Solomon's fame had not been conceived through might of arms, or conquest on the field of battle. In this he differed sharply from his father David, in fact, it is at times difficult to credit they were even related. Rather, the fame Solomon experienced was unique, and for that reason emanated from his kingdom in all directions more rapidly. He had received a special gift from his God: 'wisdom that is from above' (James 3:17).

The gift was granted when Solomon was a young man (970BC) - Josephus the Jewish historian suggests only fourteen years old (just 'a little child', 1 Kings 3:7) - and newly ascended to the throne. Desirous of receiving divine blessing upon his reign (and presenting to God as many as 1,000 burnt offerings in the process), the new king accompanied by a large number of the country's leaders and (no doubt) priests went to Gibeon, about six miles north west of Jerusalem (2 Chron.1:1-6).

That night Solomon had a dream, in which God invited him to ask for anything he wanted most (1 Kings 3:10,11). As a young man he might have been tempted to request 'riches, wealth or honour' and certainly longevity, but his reply to the challenge was pleasing to heaven. It revealed a concern for the glory of God on the one hand, and a mature grasp of covenant relationships on the other: 'Now, O Lord God, let thy promise unto David my father be established…..' (2 Chron.1:9).

That request having received the priority, and deeply aware of his royal responsibilities, Solomon proceeded to ask in his dream for 'wisdom and knowledge' (2 Chron.1:10), and 'an understanding heart' (1 Kings 3:9).

Solomon awoke to the realisation that the gift was his, in fact, his faith and devotion having been tested, God granted him much more than he had expected. As Abraham returned from the land of Moriah where he had been prepared to sacrifice Isaac, amazed that he still had his son beside him (Gen.22:12), and as 'the Lord blessed the latter end of Job more than his beginning' (Job 42:12), Solomon also experienced the divine beneficence. He had heard God promise, 'I have also given thee that which thou hast NOT asked, both riches, and honour: so that there shall not be any among the kings like unto thee all thy days' (1 Kings 3:13).

FOURFOLD WISDOM

He had asked for an understanding heart, and upon his return to Jerusalem the exercise of his brand new gift was immediately called for in a local dispute (1 Kings 3:16-28). Two harlots, each with a newly born baby, approached the young king. They shared accommodation, and during the night one of the women had accidentally suffocated her child by lying upon it. The woman accused the other of having swapped babies, replacing the dead infant with the remaining one. This was denied. So, who was telling the truth, and to which of the two women did the living baby belong? They sought the King about the matter.

It was very doubtful Josephus was correct in suggesting Solomon was only fourteen at the time, because the new king had already fathered a child (1 Kings 11:42; 14:21), but he was certainly extremely young to have to shoulder such a responsibility. It was for this reason 'all Israel' was so impressed with his decision (1 Kings 3:28). He suggested an unusual psychological ploy; that the surviving baby should be cut in half, and shared by both women! Immediately, the actual mother of the infant was horrified and was prepared to give it away, rather than that it should die.

Having proved to himself and to the nation as a whole, on a LOCAL level, that his divine gift of wisdom was genuine (1 Kings 3:28), it was now ready to be exercised NATIONALLY. The nation under Solomon's rule was about to become the most impressive in the Middle East: regally resplendent, extraordinarily prosperous, efficiently governed, and politically secure (1 Kings 4:25). Here lay some of the reasons for Solomon's widespread fame throughout the region, bringing the Queen to his front door.

Solomon took over where David left off, consolidating what his father had established through conquest. But unlike his father he lived to see the kingdom at its finest hour. Israel and Judah, whose proud citizens were 'as the sand which is by the sea in multitude' (1 Kings 4:20), stretched from 'the river (Euphrates) even unto the land of the Philistines, and to the border of Egypt' (2 Chron.9:26). Yet despite the extent of the territory, such was the genius behind Solomon's administrative skills, the impression created is of everything being at his fingertips; that nothing escaped his notice.

This was first of all achieved through the princes – his governing 'cabinet' – who together comprised a formidable company.

THE HIGH PRIEST: Zadok was high priest until the temple was built (2 Sam.8:17; 15:24), then Azariah succeeded (1 Kings 4:2). The office was held for life, Abiathar holding the title even though he had been deposed (1 Kings 2:26,27; 4:4). In New Testament times, Annas had retired but was still referred to as the high priest (Luke 3:2).

THE SCRIBES: rather than lawyers, Elihoreth and Ahiah were Secretaries of State (1 Kings 4:3). They represented the king in official matters, and issued his edicts and letters.

THE RECORDER: as already noted, Jehoshaphat (not the king of that name) had held this position in David's day (2 Sam.8:16). The job entailed analysing and preserving the nation's archives (1 Kings 4:3).

THE ARMY COMMANDER: Benaiah had been in command of the two divisions of David's bodyguards (2 Sam.8:15-18). Now promoted by the new king (1 Kings 4:4), he took over this post from his more famous predecessor Joab who had been executed for murder by Benaiah at Solomon's direct command (1 Kings 2:28-34).

THE PRIVY COUNSELLOR: Zabud (1 Kings 4:5) succeeded Hushai as Solomon's adviser, 'the king's friend' (2 Sam.15:37; 16: 16).

SUPERVISOR OF THE 'TRIBUTE': During David's reign it was Adoram (2 Sam.20:24), but who was known in Solomon's day as Adoniram (1 Kings 4:6). He could never have hoped to be popular (1 Kings 5:13-18)!

These offices had existed in his father's time, but Solomon added two more. There was Ahishar the overseer of the palace, and Azariah who was appointed 'over the officers' (1 Kings 4:5,6). It was an important post, because the nation was now divided into twelve districts (but not necessarily according to tribal boundaries), a governor ('officer') in charge of each one. Two of them were sons-in-law of the King (1 Kings 4:11,15)! Clearly nothing taking place within the nation, either the attitudes or the activities of the people, escaped the attention of the Throne.

How 'wisely' established had been this situation, when men were conscripted for hard unpaid labour (1 Kings 5:13), or when taxes were demanded. Each district – on a rota of a month a year – was expected to provide 'victuals' for Solomon's court: food for the humans, and fodder for the animals (1 Kings 4:7-28). This was no simple undertaking, EACH DAY of the week in every month, year upon year.

The provisions received at the palace were 'thirty measures of fine flour, and three-score measures of meal, ten fat oxen, and twenty oxen out of the pastures, and an hundred sheep, beside harts, and roebucks and fallowdeer, and fatted fowl' (1 Kings 4:22-28). Needless to say, the king, his courtiers and guests lacked nothing, but as a result the peoples' 'yoke' was very heavy, about which they later complained (1 Kings 12:4).

But who could say it was not worth it? Which nation in history has been so protectively overshadowed by divine favour; the people dwelling safely, 'every man under his vine and under his fig tree', from one end of the kingdom to the other (1 Kings 4:25)? They did so because the army had been ordered by royal command to permanently fortify the strategic positions through which invading forces would seek to enter: the extreme north, the north-south pass into the Esdraelon Valley, and the western approaches from Philistine territory (1 Kings 9:15-19).

In other words, surrounding the nation's heartland a protective military wall had been skilfully placed into position (2 Chron.8:4-6). The wise king, though, not only had his subjects in mind when he devised this strategy, but his own interests also, for if enemies without were kept at bay, so too were troublemakers within, as eventually proved to be the case (1 Kings 11:40).

However, Solomon's tactical skills were not only employed in negatively preventing war with his neighbours, but also in positively keeping the peace. Tragically his method, although typical of the times among royal families, involved perverted 'wisdom' displeasing to God. For example, at the commencement of his reign, Solomon aligned himself and his kingdom to the Egyptians, strangers to the covenant between God and his people (2 Chron.6:14), by marrying the Pharaoh's daughter (1 Kings 3:1). Later he extended this policy by taking wives from other neighbouring and idolatrous nations: the Ammonites, Moabites, Zidonians, Edomites and Hittites (1 Kings 11:1), and in doing so, introduced a 'multi-faith' situation to God's people.

Solomon knew only too well what damage this action would produce for his people, and hurt to their souls (1 Kings 11:6), but he 'conveniently' overlooked God's solemn command revealed through the Mosaic injunction. It referred to the likely behaviour of future monarchs (1 Kings 11:2), part of which stated, 'Neither shall he multiply wives to himself, that his heart turn not away....' (Deut.17:17). Solomon's wilful disobedience resulted in the eventual break-up of his kingdom (1 Kings 11:11; 12:1-20).

Still, on the day of the Queen's visit she would have been unaware that Solomon had offended his God. Instead like any tourist after an exhausting journey, she was only too pleased to have arrived, and safely. Jerusalem, at last! She had heard so much about this great city, the capital of a remarkable nation. Many miles, miles upon miles, of seemingly endless scrubland from one horizon to the next with a boiling sun above, but her thoughts had been elsewhere, swimming with curiosity and serious questions.

But first, her impressions: The Kingdom of Sheba, 'the land of spices', was renowned as a commercial centre of excellence, but the Queen had now more than met its match. She had arrived at the terminus of the 'incense road', from which merchants of various lands followed the caravan trails in all directions, South to Egypt, north to Phoenicia and Asia Minor, east to Syria. At the same time, back along these routes drawn in the sand was brought 'tribute' from lands conquered by David, who were still expected to pay homage to his son.

From Israel's ports, ships sailed the Red Sea and the Indian Ocean groaning under the weight of expensive cargo: gold, silver, precious stones, ivory – and exotica such as apes and peacocks. There was also what appears to have been a trading deal with Egypt, to act as 'agent' for the exporting of horses, linen and chariots for which that country was famous. Likewise for Phoenicia too where copper was the main export, as the designation 'ships of Tarshish' indicates; a phrase used for Phoenician ships transporting copper ingots from refineries in Sardinia and Cyprus (1 Kings 10:21-29). Israel mined her own copper in the Jordan Valley, and south of the Dead Sea.

God's promise then, made at the beginning of Solomon's reign, that apart from wisdom and an understanding heart he would receive 'riches, and honour', was fulfilled (1 Kings 3:13). In fact so honoured was Solomon, each time visiting dignitaries arrived, and there were many every year, they brought with them gifts fit for a sovereign (2 Chron.9:23,24): 'vessels of silver, and vessels of gold, and garments, and armour, and spices, horses, and mules', and this practice continued unceasingly as the years passed (1 Kings 10:24,25). Needless to say, the Queen of the South was no exception. The camels ambling behind her in the procession heading for the palace had been heaped high with treasures Solomon would shortly receive: 120 talents of gold, 'and of spices very great store, and precious stones....' (1 Kings 10:10).

In Jerusalem therefore the signs of great wealth and material prosperity were everywhere to be seen, and the Queen had yet to be shown the imposing buildings. Over a period of twenty years (1

Kings 9:10), no expense had been spared in erecting the finest of them in the city. First, the house of the Lord that had taken seven years to complete, and standing proudly nearby to which the Queen was heading, the exquisite palace built in almost twice the time (1 Kings 6:1,38; 7:1)!

Accompanying them were the other beautiful, but slightly less imposing edifices, including the palace built especially for Pharaoh's daughter and Solomon's favourite wife (2 Chron.8:11). There was also the house of the forest of Lebanon (Is.22:8) – supported by that land's legendary cedar trees (Ps.92:12) – used as an armoury. Then the porch of pillars ('there was not the like made in any kingdom'), where the King ascended six steps to an ivory throne overlaid with gold to judge the people (1 Kings 10:16-20). In short, Solomon was 'arrayed in glory'; opulence coupled to magnificence (Matt.6:29).

A mere glance round her would have convinced the visitor the long journey had been worthwhile, impressive indeed, but there were other matters as well which occupied her mind. Her host was concerned with very much more than commerce and architecture. The man she was about to meet was renowned for his all-embracing NATURAL wisdom, a sage to whom the high and the lowly paid their respects, and from whom they sought to learn. His fame 'was in all nations round about' (1 Kings 4:31,34).

Solomon was known therefore as one who 'excelled the wisdom of all the children of the east country, and all the wisdom of Egypt', in fact, 'wiser than all men'; a writer who under God the Holy Spirit authored his 'words of the Preacher' (Eccles.1:1), 'song of songs' (Cant.1:1), and two of the Psalms (72 and 127); a philosopher who placed on record his 3,000 proverbs (Prov.1:1); a musician who composed 1,005 songs; an intellectual with a varied and extensive knowledge, who 'spake of trees, from the cedar tree that is in Lebanon even unto the hyssop that springeth out of the wall: he spake also of beasts, and of fowl, and of creeping things, and of fishes' (1 Kings 4:32,33).

THE FOURTH DIMENSION

For a long time, across the Arabian desert had circulated accounts about this remarkable man, King Solomon, but were they not exaggerated? Jerusalem was far away from Marib, and stories are often embellished with constant re-telling, it therefore seemed unlikely to the Queen that what she had heard was reliable (1 Kings 10:7). And yet.... There was something fascinating her more than anything else, enough for her to insist upon undertaking such an epic journey fraught with danger.

Curiosity alone would not have drawn her such a distance. A delegate could have satisfied her in discovering the truth. No, it was imperative she met Solomon personally, because the issue was so important only a face-to-face meeting with him could satisfy her heart and mind. The questions she wished to ask were numerous, and she believed only Solomon could answer them for her (1 Kings 10:1).

The fact was she had become aware of a fourth dimension to Solomon's astonishing gifts, a mysterious secret, what centuries later would be referred to as 'the WISDOM of God in a mystery, even the HIDDEN WISDOM, which God ordained before the world....' (1 Cor.2:7). It was that thrilling realisation which had brought her to Jerusalem from 'the uttermost part of the earth' (Matt.12:42), in the hope of learning it. Solomon was now within reach, but would he tell her? She would soon find out.

TWO
First Meeting

Upon arrival at the palace, after so long and arduous a journey, one can safely assume the Queen would not have been ushered into the King's presence immediately. The preliminary courtesies of a gracious host had first to be observed, the honoured guest and her large entourage being shown their spacious apartments by court officials and those in attendance. Time was required for rest and the settling in to a new and strange environment, before the meeting with Solomon could take place, and the agenda of official engagements set in motion.

How long she waited – for the presence of an absolute monarch is never approached hurriedly – is unknown. Perhaps it was several days. Whatever the time span, with her eagerness to meet him it could not have been a simple matter to wait. Still, before doing so, she had ample time to marvel at her surroundings. The impressive architecture, sumptuous décor, lavish hospitality, generous provision (2 Chron.9:4): these, together with the elegance of the court officials and the orderliness of the palace servants, no doubt produced admiration from all the visitors, and certainly from Sheba herself

(1Kings 10:5). Evidently, the palace was not only decoratively exquisite, but also efficiently managed.

Everywhere the guests looked gold stared back at them. One should not be surprised. After all, Solomon's coffers were filled to the brim with the 666 talents of it placed annually in his treasury, apart from many other sources of income (1 Kings 10:14,15). And now his latest visitor had contributed still more, 'gold in abundance, and precious stones' (2 Chron.9:1).

INITIAL IMPRESSIONS

Biblical history has recorded the names of many notable people, but those of 'Solomon and Sheba' are among the most famous; the fascination of preachers, historians, archeologists, scholars of various kinds and academia in general – as well as romantic novelists and the inevitable movie-makers. All have a desire to paint their own scenario of what took place that eventful moment when the two first met.

Not long before, during the temple's official opening ceremony, Solomon had prayerfully prophesied of 'a stranger, that is not of thy people Israel, but cometh out of a far country for thy name's sake' (1 Kings 8:41), but probably he had not considered that the stranger would be a woman. Some time would elapse before his descendants had a female reign over them (2 Kings 11:3), it must therefore have come as a surprise to hear of the approach of the QUEEN of the Kingdom of Sheba. But for that reason, even before meeting her, Solomon must surely have been impressed. Intrigued too, a king journeying all that way, but a queen?

Just how impressed the King was the recorder makes clear, because shortly afterwards Solomon was not only eager to supply his royal guest with the answers to her 'hard' questions (1 Kings 10:1), but significantly was willing to give her 'whatsoever she asked' (2 Chron.9:12). Such generosity was surely not available to ALL of the King's guests, even the royal ones! But whether the two were romantically linked during this period together (there is a Jewish school which believes they were) is only conjecture and immaterial to the major theme of the story.

In the meantime, the famous moment arrived. They had been unseen trading partners, probably for a long time their names very familiar to each other, but now here they were together in the same room. Two remarkable people, the King of Israel exceeding all others in wealth and wisdom (1 Kings 10:23) and the Queen of Sheba who like Solomon, centuries later the Son of God himself considered worth mentioning (Matt.6:29; 12:42).

What thoughts were theirs upon first sight of each other, needless to say, are unknown. However, an intelligent guess can easily be made. From the Queen's point of view, behind the grandeur of majesty and doubtless her appearance of regal serenity, there lay a troubled soul. Solomon's glorious kingdom was impressive to say the least, his noted wit and wisdom intriguing, and fresh trading agreements between Israel and Sheba were important – but above everything else, she was anxious to 'commune' with him about far weightier matters (2 Chron.9:1). These had been on her mind for a long time, when alone within her palace at Marib, and as she crossed the Arabian desert heading for Jerusalem.

So, what was Sheba thinking when she was ushered into Solomon's presence? When longing to express profound and heart-felt issues to somebody one believes can help, especially after many miles to do so, there can only be a tremendous sense of relief that at last the burden is about to be shed. But would it be? She had no way of knowing. As a monarch of the ancient world she, of all people, would appreciate the despotic nature of royal decisions. She was in no position to say to him, 'what doest thou? (Eccles. 8:4)'.

If she had arrived in Jerusalem uninvited, as appears to have been the case (1 Kings 10:1), there was no guarantee he could be persuaded to satisfy her quest. After all, she would have known hers was not the only visit to have been made from afar, as 'all the kings of the earth sought the presence of Solomon, to hear his wisdom, that God had put in his heart' (2 Chron.9:23). It might well be, that as far as HE was concerned here was yet another visitor, a queen this time! But then, SHE may have thought, would not that fact work to her advantage? In the light of what happened following her visit, the influx of many foreign women invited into Israel (1 Kings 11:1), if that had been the Queen's thinking no doubt she was correct.

As for Solomon: even before she entered his presence he must have been intrigued, but was also probably very wary of her. She was a woman! As everyone now knows, the King had a weakness for women, his palace complex eventually filled to the brim with 700 wives, and his harem with 300 concubines. 1,000 women, who had 'turned away' a vulnerable heart (1 Kings 11:13), and his latest guest was a female who had travelled – and at such a sacrifice to her safety – just to seek an audience with him!

So, what did he really know about his guest, this dark-skinned lady standing before him? Very little, except by repute; that HER kingdom was a beautiful place, pervaded by the aroma of sweet spices, and that HIS kingdom had prospered by trading with her, but apart from that, virtually nothing. As a queen she would certainly have had the appearance of an honourable and 'gracious woman' (Prov.11:16), but was she to be trusted? Was her heart 'snares and nets' (Eccles.7:26), and would her lips 'drop as an honeycomb' because her mouth was 'smoother than oil' (Prov.5: 3)? Solomon of all people was aware of the temptations he faced, although it seems he had succumbed to them all, of how easily his guest could deceive him, a possibility he found 'more bitter than death' (Eccles.7:26).

Why had she come? To Solomon the answer seemed obvious. Was it not to strengthen and widen trade agreements, to search for the truth behind the rumours she had heard, to discover the source of his wisdom, to put it to the test by delighting in asking numerous questions? He probably hoped they would not be silly ones; 'guesses, riddles, witty and ingenious conceits' as one Bible Encyclopaedia suggests. If 'all the earth', as it were, wanted to hear Solomon's wisdom (1 Kings 10:24), there must have been occasions when the visitors overlooked the fact that he was a very busy man! Did not the King sigh now-and-then at the wasting of his precious time? He must have wondered initially whether this visit by the Queen was one of them; whether her 'multitude of words' would denote that she was a foolish woman (Eccles.5:3).

AN UNEASY PRESENCE

It could not have been straightforward conversing with Solomon, because his wisdom included an extraordinary gift for shrewdness.

Wisdom given 'from above' always does (James 3: 17). His spiritual discernment and perception of others' qualities would have been razor-sharp (1 Kings 3:9,28); his guests made uncomfortable by this realisation.

Even as they asked their questions, they were aware they were exposing their true selves in the light of his penetrating gaze. The Queen was no exception. She was learning from him, but he was also learning from her, because 'a wise man will hear, and will increase learning' (Prov.1:5). The sincerity of her questioning, the quality of her questions, her body language: these all told their stories about her, and what materialised was that although Solomon was not one to 'suffer fools gladly' (2 Cor.11:9), the Queen of the South could hold her head high. She was clearly no fool.

That is, on any level, but particularly in the way Solomon understood the word. It is a special one, more prominent in the divine vocabulary (or should be) than in man's. In other words, the description 'fool' possesses a theological (1 Cor.15:35,36) as well as a spiritual (Ps.14:1) connotation, and therefore not to be used lightly or angrily. 'Hell fire' awaits those who do, promised One greater than Solomon (Matt.5:22; 12:42).

Inspired by God the Spirit (2 Tim.3:16), the Spirit of truth (John 16:13), as Jesus drives the widest of wedges between 'flesh' and 'spirit' (John 3:6), Solomon underlines the demarcation separating heaven's revelation and that which opposes it: a sharp distinction, an enormous gulf. Thus, the battle lines are drawn. On the one side is 'the Lord', and in his team are 'wisdom', 'knowledge', 'understanding', 'instruction', 'righteousness' etc. But the opposing side is captained by 'the fool' (in whom God has no 'pleasure', Eccles.5:4): 'the wicked', 'the scorner', 'the proud' etc. And the opposition is fierce ('fools despise wisdom', Prov.1: 7), not surprisingly, because 'the fear of the Lord is the beginning of knowledge' (Prov.1:7), and equally 'knowledge of the holy is understanding' (Prov.9:10).

In his visiting guest, then, Solomon recognised a thirsting soul desirous of being on the right side of the divide. Or as Another declared, 'Blessed are they which hunger and thirst after righteousness, for they shall be filled' (Matt.5:6).

THE TIE THAT BINDS

On one occasion, a reply to a question produced a delighted response, 'Thou art not far from the kingdom of God' (Mark 12: 34). Likewise, it was this aspect of things that excited Solomon about Sheba, not sensuality but spirituality. His acute sensitivity to the state of another's soul would have informed him there was every reason to be encouraged.

He surely knew 'deep down' her visit had nothing to do with trivia or mere curiosity (and how bored he must often have been by those seeking only to be entertained), nor was it ultimately about trade. Commerce was obviously important to the Queen, indeed vital for her country, but there was something much more wonderful and fascinating she hankered after. This yearning had compelled her, at great risk, to traverse a dangerous desert in search of the spiritual oasis in Jerusalem. Spiritual people will empathise with her, and also share in Solomon's joy at recognising the signs. God had provided Sheba with questions and the determination to have them answered, and equally, she had been irresistibly drawn to Solomon as her teacher. She just HAD to have her soul satisfied.

It would have been soon evident to Solomon this was the correct assessment. Sheba's questions were not of passing interest, gossamer-thin, casually sought after. They were 'hard', profound (1 Kings 10:1). She was in earnest, not merely sitting in silence listening to a monologue, but 'communing' with Solomon 'of all that was in her heart' (2 Chron.9:1). ALL, nothing excluded, and to a virtual stranger! It was evident a remarkable rapport had built up between them, which has brought 'Solomon and Sheba' to history's attention. Regal reticence was swept aside, protocol forgotten, as a burdened soul unloaded itself upon a listening ear.

But what was it that Solomon so desired to teach, and Sheba was so eager to learn? Like Mary sitting beside Jesus hanging upon his every word (Luke 10:39), or the enthusiastic primitive church being taught by the apostles about nine centuries later (Acts 2:41, 42), the two monarchs were engrossed in matters 'CONCERNING THE NAME OF THE LORD' (1 Kings 10:1), and can there be a more enthralling subject? To catch a glimpse of God's 'name'

(Exod.3:13,14) is to touch the hem of heaven; to 'know' him (John 17:3), and to have observed 'the mysteries of the kingdom' unveiled (Matt.13:11): in short, to have been born anew (John 3:7).

With Solomon as her guide Sheba had embarked upon a great theological and spiritual adventure, a privilege almighty God grants only to a minority (Matt.20:16) in each generation (Exod.33: 19). After all 'the deep' (Dan.2:22) and 'secret things' (Deut.29: 29) are his – as also are ' WISDOM and might' (Dan.2:20) – and he alone reveals them (Rom.9:15,16). Sheba would therefore have had conveyed to her, in embryo, 'the revelation of the mystery, which was kept secret since the world began' (Rom.16:25).

THE MEETING OF MINDS

So, where could the quest begin?

Every pioneer missionary can relate to Solomon's difficulty. On the one hand, his religious pedigree was not only impressive to his guest, but awesome too. Solomon was the king of the mighty nation of Israel, renowned for its magnificence throughout vast territories of envying neighbours, that claimed to have been the recipient of the oracles of the one true God (Rom.3:2).

Within that nation Solomon was rooted in the Abrahamic covenant (Gen.12:1-3), of the messianic (Rev.5:5) tribe of Judah (Gen.49:8-12), a member of the choice family of David (2 Sam.7: 16), of whom the Creator himself testified he was a man after his own heart (Acts 13:22). By contrast, Sheba's kingdom could only boast an ornate temple to Ilumquh the moon god! Clearly, although she was eager to learn, she also had great heights to reach.

Solomon's answer to the problem appears to have been twofold. First, in the learning process, he encouraged her to use her eyes as well as her ears. Issues relating to 'the name of the Lord' (1 Kings 10:1) are never solely academic, confined only to the lecture hall, but rather are primarily experiential. She was HEARING his replies to her questions (2 Chron.9:2), but she was also obliged to OBSERVE; that what he had been teaching her was clearly reflected in God's blessings upon the nation. Thus, in the process of her enquiries, Sheba at the same time saw for herself 'the house that he had built, and the meat of his table, and the sitting of his servants, and the attendance of the ministers, and their apparel, and his cupbearers'. But, undoubtedly, the most important of all 'his ascent by which he went up unto the house of the Lord' (1 Kings 10:3-5).

Then secondly, Solomon was not content for Sheba to be merely a student asking questions, or a quiet and observant spectator. He would have wanted to build a bridge, a point of contact, to bring them closer together in order to make it easier for him to communicate the truth, and for her to understand it. But was it possible? Not only were their countries far apart, separated geographically by a millennium of miles, but also did not the religious and cultural differences make a meeting of minds impossible?

At first it would have appeared so, but Solomon knew otherwise. Sheba may have known it before she left Marib, perhaps encouraging her to leave the comforts of her palace and head for Jerusalem, but then again she might have been ignorant of the facts. Whichever was the case, if the latter, her teacher was about to astonish her. It was the strongest of 'bridges'. He informed - or reminded her– that they were related! Distantly so, it is true, but related nevertheless.

A COMMON SOURCE

Actually, she probably DID know and wanted to learn more about this intriguing story. It was a good reason for meeting Solomon. It would also explain why a foreigner was anxious to enquire about Solomon's 'Lord' (1 Kings 10:1). Perhaps aspects of Israel's history featured somewhere within her country's folklore. As Israel's citizens understood why they were called 'Israelites' (Gen.32:28), surely those of the Queen's realm also knew something about the origin of THEIR country. If so, then they would appreciate that far beyond their reach – over distant horizons (Matt.12:42) – there existed a land whose history they shared. In any case, accounts of the miraculous powers of the Israelites' Deity had been circulating the heathen nations for many years (Josh.2: 10).

But which part of that history was shared? There were three periods from which to choose. First was that which followed the catastrophic upheaval caused by the worldwide flood, when a family of eight descended from the ark (Gen.8:18). From this origin the earth was replenished. Noah was the head of this family, and his three sons were progenitors of nations: Shem of the olive skinned peoples, Ham of the dark skinned, and Japheth the 'father' of the fair (Gen.9:1).

A view held by Josephus was that as the inhabitants of Sheba's kingdom were descendants of Ham – a 'Sheba' being Ham's great grandson (Gen.10:6-20) – the Queen had not travelled to Jerusalem from the southern region of the Arabian desert, but rather from 'the tabernacles of Ham' (Ps.78:51): Egypt. Hence, Josephus refers to Solomon's royal guest not as reigning over 'the land of spices', but as the Queen of Egypt.

The story though is much more complex than that, a fact which introduces the second historical period. Egypt was undoubtedly 'the land of Ham' (Ps.105:23), but antiquity records that the people of Ham were also to be found in the vicinity of the Tigris and the Euphrates. That is, the region of the Persian Gulf, as well as the peninsula of what is now known as Arabia. However, very early (2000BC) a large portion of the Semitic peoples – Shem's family – migrated from Asian territory and infiltrated the race of Ham. God had permitted it. The sin of Ham's son had been the reason why Ham was disowned. As a result he was known merely as 'the father of Canaan' (Gen.9:20-26), the son whose sin against his grandfather Noah had provoked the divine judgment.

It is not surprising then to discover a 'Sheba', although descended from Ham, residing with his family among the people of Shem (Gen.10:7,21,28). A map depicting the tribal areas of that period reveals 'Sheba' occupying the centre of Arabia, the 'travelling companies' of his brother 'Dedan' the south west (Is.21: 13), and those of 'Havilah' another brother the north west (Gen.10: 7; Ezek.38:13). The prophet Ezekiel also associates 'Sheba' and his father Raamah with the land of 'all spices' (27:22).

However, as Shem's family enlarged it was obliged to enter more fertile lands to all points north of Arabia, bringing the Shemitic (Semitic) nations into being: Ammonites, Arameans, Assyrians, Babylonians, Edomites, Moabites, Phoenicians – and of course the

Hebrews, who were descended from Eber (Gen.10:21), from whom eventually Abraham came (Gen.11:14-26).

AN APPETITE WHETTED

With the reference to the mighty Patriarch, the historic pattern having taken shape and the final piece of the jig-saw about to be placed into position, probably the first of the Queen's 'hard' questions was being excitingly answered.

Sarah had died (Gen.23:1,2), and her husband Abraham remarried. His new wife was Keturah, and the union produced six sons. Eventually, grandchildren were born and a 'Sheba' was among them (Gen 25:1-3). And from where did his grandmother Keturah originate? According to some scholars, including Josephus - Arabia!

In the unfolding of his story Solomon had built his 'bridge', his point of contact with the Queen. In Abraham they and their subjects were related. If for this information, or confirmation, alone Sheba knew her sojourn had been worthwhile. She may have suspected the truth, but now it had been told her first hand from one whose wisdom was renown. However, this was only the beginning of her quest, a basis for discussion: a springboard from which deeper and even more enthralling lessons were to be learned. She had a long way to go, but what adventurous thoughts the Lord's 'name' conjured up for her!

SECTION
ONE

'...get thee into the land of Moriah...'
(Gen. 22:2)

THREE
Highest in the Heavens

How quickly circumstances change! One moment Solomon and Sheba were strangers, over 1,000 miles apart, and the next were delighting in the fellowship a newly cemented relationship brings. Reserve on both sides was swept aside as she opened her heart to him, and he in return unravelled her queries (1 Kings 10:2,3).

Their ancestry then had a common source: Abraham. He through Sarah (1 Peter 3:6), and she in Keturah (Gen.25:1-3). Like one who has discovered a long-lost relative, Sheba must have been brim-full with contrasting emotions: excitement, curiosity, and eagerness, impatience too, she understanding so little, and having so much to learn. The questions must have breathtakingly tumbled from her. But where was she to begin?

The mention of Abraham would have opened up a wealth of historical and spiritual treasures. The Patriarch was one of the gigantic pillars of the Israelite nation, a pivotal figure, whose presence was felt everywhere the people trod (Gen.12:1-3). That silhouette still looms over the Church, where revealed truth (1 Tim.3:15) and true faith are found (Gal.3:9). Solomon's wisdom therefore had to bring order to what was possibly a plethora of disjointed questioning.

So, where would his starting point have been? A clue is provided within the text. Sheba had travelled a very long way because she was attracted by 'the name of the Lord' (1 Kings 10:1). That being so, before his 'name' could be known and understood the first questions asked would surely have been about Jehovah himself. In which case, it would have proved a refreshing experience for Sheba, after many years spent under the influence of the moon god! Especially, as Solomon's father had eulogised the 'Lord' for deftly creating the moon with a mere touch of his 'fingers' (Ps.8:3)!

CONTRASTS

That surely was the first surprise – if not shock – Sheba received, the experience every soul undergoes when drawn from heathenism to true worship (John 4:24). A sudden realisation overwhelms, and mankind's greatest tragedy confronted, that one's 'sign post' has always been pointing in the wrong direction. What one considered 'sight' is in fact blindness (John 9:40,41), and the 'truth' about which one was assured is nothing but error (Is.55:8). How humbling the awareness is, perhaps humiliating, to have had exposed the deadness of one's soul (Ephes.2:1).

Then again, Sheba could not help but contrast herself with Solomon. With what assurance he ascended the temple steps (1 Kings 10:5), but how uncertain was she of her own beliefs, that a desert was traversed seeking truth in a foreign land. He fixed his eyes on the Highest, his heart in heaven, she not high enough, no higher than the moon. Solomon had never seen his God, and yet by faith never ceased from 'seeing' him (Heb.11:27). She could see the moon, but only at certain periods, when the clouds permitted it. He worshipped in the light of grace; she worshipped in the darkness of night. Oh, how mighty is God, and yet how minute is god!

THE 'MOST HIGH' GOD

Had Sheba been present on that wonderful occasion, the inauguration of temple worship in Jerusalem (1 Kings 8), she would have understood just how mighty Solomon believed Jehovah to be.

With Ilumquh in mind it would probably have alarmed her - 'there is no God like thee, in heaven above, or on earth beneath' (1 Kings 8:23) – although she could not have helped but be impressed by what she witnessed. The King had stood before his subjects within the temple precincts, and gazing heavenwards with arms outstretched, with deep reverence he had addressed One whose majesty is such 'the heaven and heaven of heavens cannot contain' him (1 Kings 8:27).

Shortly before, Solomon's father had also prayed in a similar manner, his spirit elevated to great heights: 'Blessed be thou, Lord God of Israel our father, for ever and ever. Thine, O Lord is the greatness, and the power, and the glory, and the victory, and the majesty: for all that is in the heaven and in the earth is thine; thine is the kingdom, O Lord, and thou art exalted as head above all. Both riches and honour come of thee, and thou reignest over all; and in thine hand is power and might.... (1 Chron.29:10-13)'.

What a remarkable belief, an extraordinary concept, Sheba had every reason to think who was a stranger to these things. She must have been taken aback upon hearing the truth for the first time, as at home there was nothing to equal or even compare with it. There the deity possessed eyes which were unseeing, ears unhearing, a mouth incapable of speech, heartless and uncaring (Ps.115:4-7). It was even unable to walk and had to be carried to the plinth by the adherents, where no doubt it was held in place by nails (Jer.10:5)!

The Israelites were indeed privileged to worship a LIVING God (Ps.42:2), for whom even the vastness of eternity cannot cater. Nothing greater can be envisaged, an absolute supremacy; the Lord of heaven and earth (Matt.11:25), without equal (Is.40:25), or rivals (Is.42:8). Truly, those who worship the King of eternity (Jer. 10:10) do so joyfully, crying 'Let the Lord be magnified' (Ps.35: 27).

He sees everything, all of the time, for good or ill; hears the faintest whisper and secret thought (Ps.139:1-12); an independent Sovereign (Deut.6:4), whose giant hand is a resting place for the few (John 10:29), and a fist for the many (Rev.19:15). And even more wonderful, he SPEAKS (John 1:1)!

A deity who is omnipresent and omniscient yet cannot, or will not, communicate to his creatures is a fearful being. No words of warning, comfort, or even rebuke: only deeply frozen aloofness. By contrast, as Solomon's ancestors testified, 'For who is there of all flesh, that hath heard the voice of the living God speaking out of the midst of the fire, as we have, and lived? (Deut.5:24-26)'

Sheba, like all who quest after 'seeing him who is invisible' (Heb.11:27), was surely breathless with excitement. And as Abraham was 'father' to them both, Solomon undoubtedly told her everything recorded about the Patriarch's life (a subject for another book, Gen.11-25), and she certainly would have questioned Solomon closely about all the details of it. But the theme of greatest interest to Sheba, was Abraham's relationship to the Divine, whom he had referred to as 'the most high God, the possessor of heaven and earth' (Gen.14: 22).

A SUDDEN TRANSFORMATION

Although stories, both traditional and imaginary, might have been found within her country's folklore, there was an aspect of Abraham's life Sheba probably knew nothing about. Or, had she known, would certainly not have understood; namely, the astonishing truth that the Patriarch was not only familiar with 'the name of the Lord', but had actually met the Lord himself on a number of occasions. Sheba could have hardly waited to learn more.

First of all, to her undoubted amazement, she discovered there were similarities between Abraham's experience and her own. Whilst in the SOUTH where idols were plentiful she had UNKNOWINGLY 'met' the Lord. It had been he who had prompted her to visit the Promised Land that she might learn about him. Likewise, whilst in the EAST 'serving other gods' (Josh.24: 2), her 'father' had KNOWINGLY met that same Lord and he too was directed to the land of Promise (Gen.12:1). It was one of the most remarkable events in an equally remarkable life.

Abram, as he was then known, lived quietly and prosperously within the empire of Mesopotamia. Even though he and his family were descended from Shem (Gen.11:10-26), the land of his birth was under the control of the race of Ham (Gen.10: 10). The Semitic migrants from the south, among whom there was an understanding of true worship (Gen.9:26), did not arrive in the east until the Patriarch was 169 years old (2000BC). That is, six years before his death (1994BC) (Gen.25:7). Therefore, not knowing any better the family was idolatrous (Josh.24:2).

Then suddenly heaven burst into time and changed the entire world. What occurred is swathed in mystery, but the fact remains Abram was visited by One whom Stephen of the Christian church many centuries later described as 'the God of glory' (Acts 7:2), and Moses less formally as 'the Lord' (Gen.12:1). Either way, he not only manifested his presence to the Patriarch but actually spoke to him.

Within a few unique moments in a wealthy idolater's life an extraordinary covenant was established, which thousands of years later is still referred to as the Old Covenant. Also, two great nations were conceived that day: the Jewish nation (Gen.12:1-3), and 'the Israel of God' (Gal.6:16), the Christian Church.

But, as Abram's experience is fundamental to an understanding of both the Jewish as well as the Christian faith, it is surely not idle curiosity to seek further information into what happened. Solomon's questioner would certainly have done so. After all, it was one of the most unique experiences known to man. One moment Abram and his entire family were enjoying a very comfortable and settled life in the Chaldean city of Ur, which nestled securely within the great empire of Mesopotamia, and the next they had pulled up their roots and moved out to unknown territory and to an equally unknown future. Gone were their idols, because like Christians of a later age, they now served 'the living and true God' (1 Thess.1:9). Clearly, something very remarkable had taken place, which Sheba would have wanted to know all about.

The manifestation itself was not to the family as a whole, but to just one member of it, and where he was when it took place and what he was doing is unknown. It is of no consequence. It is enough to say, that religiously he was 'dead' to any other form of worship than to his idols; 'without God in this world' (Ephes.2:12). Needless to say, he did not possess a Bible or inspired teaching to prepare him for what happened. Nor like the future prophet (1 Sam. 3:4) or the future apostle (Acts 9:4) did he just hear a voice. That experience alone would have brought him to his knees, like the disciples on the occasion of their Lord's 'transfiguration' (Matt. 17:6).

Suddenly, without warning, no doubt with the swiftness of a wink (1 Cor.15:52), the future Patriarch was involved in a situation far beyond an understanding, or any previous experience. A rare brilliance, a startling radiance, confronted him. He would have needed to shield his eyes, for they could not have gazed at such glory. In later years, another great man who met with 'the God of glory' (Acts 7:2) was obliged to wear a veil after the encounter, because his face reflected the holiness of the divine presence, which others close to him could not bear to see (Exod.34:33-35). It is surely possible that Abram's appearance was also unusually transformed, which was reason enough for his family to believe him when he insisted they had to leave everything and head for the unknown (Heb.11:8).

The shock the seventy year old received was immense (Gen.12:4). Six centuries later, when the Israelites witnessed the glory of the Lord on Mount Sinai, they saw what looked like 'devouring fire' (Exod.24:17). But then they were watching from afar. Abram was close at hand, and without any preparation, or even a warning for what at first was a terrible ordeal. A gasp of amazement was followed by the mind seeking to receive the appropriate message from the brain. No idol was this! Dead religious observance had suddenly been cast aside, and a vibrant force substituted for it.

But Abram had not only met with dazzling glory, but with God! 'The GOD of glory appeared' (Acts 7:2). Yet, upon earth it is impossible to actually see him (1 John 4:12). Even Moses was forbidden to see God's face, just the 'back parts' of the divine being (Exod.33:23). Then who did Abram see? From behind his hands shielding his eyes, through the brightness of white light, he saw the figure of a man. It was the apostle John's experience on Patmos Isle (Rev.1:12-18), and Abram's introduction to the Lord (Gen.12:1), One whom he would meet many times again.

ENCOUNTERING A MYSTERY

Whether Sheba had heard this account before, or not, it never fails to fascinate. Who was the man reflected in the glory? It was he whom Moses heard speaking from the midst of flame (Exod.3:2), the Angel (Exod.14:19) who triumphantly led the Israelites from Egyptian bondage (Exod.13:18-22); the Warrior, his sword drawn, whom Joshua encountered on the eve of battle (Josh. 5:13-15), and the Encourager of the despondent Gideon (Judg.6: 12). In short, the One whose presence caused Samson's father to exclaim, 'We shall surely die, because we have seen God' (Judg. 13:22).

What Abram, Moses, Joshua, Gideon, Manoah, and about two million others had in common (Exod.12:37) – and even Nebuchadnezzar, who saw for himself a form within fire 'like the Son of God' (Dan.3:24,25) – was their experience of divine mystery. They were involved in a paradox, seeing One who is invisible (Heb.11:27); a 'theophanic' manifestation, the appearance of the pre-existent Christ (1 Cor.10:4), the Second Person of the Trinity: God the Son (John 1:1-5).

GOD WHO TALKS, AND WALKS

Needless to say, Abram had no idea what had happened, and in a moment of shock, guessing was beyond him. Like the apostle John in a similar situation he probably fell trembling at the Figure's feet (Rev.1:17). How could he have remained standing, or be other than speechless? But if Abram's lips were frozen, after the initial numbness, his thoughts must have tumbled one upon another. Who was this Person? What was it all about? Was judgment, or consolation, the reason for his visit?

But then, having descended from Shem, one particular thought must have loomed larger than the others in Abram's astonished mind: Shem's father Noah and the flood, 367 years earlier (cf Gen.11-12:4). The history of the Semitic peoples was well known to Moses, whom God the Spirit employed to author the book of Genesis, centuries earlier therefore Abram was surely equally familiar with it.

Would not Noah have received a similar experience? How would he have been able to 'walk with God' without one? (Gen. 6:9) The expression is both fascinating and significant. Christians spiritualise it, referring to themselves as 'walking with the Lord', but for Adam,

Eve, Enoch (Gen.5:22), Noah, Abram, Moses, Joshua, Gideon, Manoah etc, it was meant literally. They heard the voice of God, but they also saw the Person of the pre-existent Christ, and were literally able to walk alongside him (Amos 3:3).

In Eden's garden, for example, Adam and Eve heard the voice of the Lord God, but he was also 'WALKING in the garden in the cool of the day'. Why did they try and hide from his 'presence', if he was unable to be seen? (Gen.3:8) Again, in the account of the flood and the building of the ark, God the Spirit draws an interesting distinction. He wants the reader to know, that although 'God' prepared Noah for the impending judgment (Gen.6: 13-22), it was 'the Lord' who invited he and his family into the ark. Then the reader notes, significantly, did not leave it to Noah to batten down the hatches, but carried out the task himself (Gen.7:1,16). It was the ultimate security for the little family hidden inside the ark, launching out on an extraordinary adventure, the waters ominously rising. How encouraged they must have been by that gracious gesture; an assurance of their safety throughout the impending perils (Gen.7:17-24).

The flood in Noah's day was a worldwide judgment of epic proportions. Multitudes perished, a mere eight souls rescued (2 Peter 2:5). It was a catastrophe so immense that today's equally sinful mankind prefers to believe it never happened! A strong delusion indeed (2 Thess.2:11). Yet, with the subsiding of the waters, hope appeared in the form of the rainbow covenant (Rev. 4:3; 10:1), the divine promise that a worldwide flood would never be repeated (Gen.9:8-17).

A STARTLING EXPERIENCE

Now with the appearance once more of the God of glory (Acts 7;2), the Lord (Gen.12:1), another focal point in history had been reached. Abram, being human and having kept company with idols (Josh.24:2) for 75 years (Gen.12:4), was too overcome for speech, but nevertheless, in silence he was about to witness the declaration of an even more important covenant (Gen.12:1-3).

His introduction to the true God was an unusual one. At first glance he could have had no idea who the Stranger was. No announcement was made, as when the apostle John was confronted by him on Patmos Isle (Rev.1:11), and the old apostle had an advantage over the old patriarch, having known Christ albeit many years before. But the glorious appearing was a sufficient credential to one descended from Shem's family, with many traditional accounts of Noah's experience emanating from that source (Gen. 11:10-32).

But not only was the appearance unannounced, Abram was not greeted either (Gen.12:1). In future generations those taken unawares by eternity, when abject fear was understandably the instinctive reaction, were pacified upon hearing their names being called (Exod.3:4; 1 Sam.3:6; John 20:16), or at least, receiving other comforting assurances (Luke 2:10). But not Abram: instead, the first words he heard was a command, and one which would not only have puzzled him, but would also have severely challenged him (Gen.12:1).

The absence of preliminaries served a useful purpose, emphasising the importance of what was about to be declared. What kind of man receives so vital a covenant? He had to discover for himself. Thus, the ingredients of the old covenant came later, the Lord's priority was the testing of the old man. Therefore, whereas Noah was invited to look UPWARDS at the beautiful covenantal rainbow arch, AFTER the mighty deluge associated with him (Gen.9:13), Abram was constrained to look INWARDS at himself, PRIOR to the giving of the covenant (Gen. 12:1).

It was the unexpected which would at first have puzzled Abram; in an instance facing the startling contrast between 'serving other gods' (Josh.24:2), and then hearing 'the true God' (Jer.10:10) commanding him without any warning that he was to make a great personal sacrifice. He had lived in Mesopotamia for three quarters of a century (Gen.12:4), the home where his roots were; his culture, religion, family, property and friends. Yet he was being ordered to venture forth into the unknown, in fact, to a foreign land beyond the Mesopotamian borders, where he and his family had never set foot before.

He would understandably have been mystified. The information given him was in short supply, a bare minimum to whet the appetite. He had been stripped of any dependence upon manufactured props: organisational skills in readiness for what lay ahead, navigational expertise for the journey, or reasoned arguments against his attempting the trip in the first place. Only trust in the Stranger's veracity was left to him, that (in another context) 'what he had promised, he was able to perform' (Rom.4: 21).

But Abram not being a robot, many were the questions that surely entered his mind. Where was this country to which he must go? What dangers would he face? Where would he live? Many questions, but no answers were given, just the realisation that God had to be trusted without question, and without questions. Had he not been assured of his new acquaintance's companionship? He had promised Abram he would 'show' him the territory of his adoption (Gen.12:1), and as there were no brochures or photographs available, this could only mean that the most welcomed of all Companions would accompany him (Prov.18:24).

But being prepared to make the journey was even more difficult than at first it appeared. Obeying this glorious Being, trusting him implicitly, heading towards an unknown future: these things Abram was willing to do, but what about his family? How would they react, and particularly his wife Sarai? The command to leave Chaldea had surely included her, God not likely to separate them (Gen.2:24; Matt.19:5). But supposing she refused to leave home, relatives and friends? What then? After all, in fathoming matters divine, she did not always keep in step with her husband (Gen.18:10-15). It must have been the worst possible scenario Abram could have imagined. Nevertheless, whatever else happened, HE would have to obey, because an encounter with God can never be made a secondary issue.

Having suffered the shock of the sudden appearance of the Stranger, and the unexpected challenge which immediately followed it, Abram had scarcely caught his breath when he heard the positive side of the Visitor's message. It astonished him still further.

Until that point the message had been negative; that he had to forsake the old in preference for the new – culture, kindred, country and even his religion. Now, though, he learned an important principle in his newfound relationship with the true and living God. Unlike his idols, which only ever received but never gave, God always generously replenishes those who sacrifice at his insistence (Matt.19:27-30). Abram had been commanded to leave behind him a great deal he held dear, but to fill the vacuum he would receive blessings far beyond what he could dream about.

MOMENTOUS PROMISES

What he heard were seven brief statements, but his attention was surely drawn to the two words introducing them: 'I WILL' (Gen.12:2,3). There was an unusual ring to it. Even if his gods had been capable of speech, having 'mouths' which never opened (Ps. 115:5), could Abram have envisaged them being able to use the expression? The words, 'I will' uttered by Deity denote a sovereign purpose (Ephes.1:11), one which his gods clearly did not possess. In fact he would now have to agree with the prophet Jeremiah, who many centuries later in a scathing denunciation of idolatry, described idols as 'upright as the palm tree, but speak not: they must needs be borne, because they cannot go' (Jer.10:5).

But now the phrase 'I WILL' had provided a proper perspective to Abram's situation. Gone were the days of selfish independence, the prosperous landowner ruler of his domestic gods, as he was of all he surveyed (Gen.31:34). Now he no longer held A 'deity' in his hand, but THE Deity held him (John 10:29); no more was he the governor of his gods, but the governed by God (Is.40:21-31). Clearly, in an instance, a radical transformation in Abram's life had taken place.

THE QUEST FOR MORE

There is little doubt that this facet of Abram's experience would have delighted Solomon to relate to the Queen, some of whose 'hard questions' were surely connected to this subject. Those who can claim the Patriarch as their ancestor, whether racially (Josh.24:2,3) or spiritually (Rom.4), always rejoice in recalling that extraordinary moment when the Old Covenant was first made known. Having discovered, or been reminded of the fact, that Abram was also her 'father', the subject would have excited Sheba too. If this God had delivered HIM from idolatry, could he not do the same for HER?

So, Abram's Visitor having delivered his instructions, what were the remarkable blessings promised? Although Sheba may have already known them, she would nevertheless have wanted to know more – and Solomon was only too willing to oblige.

FOUR
Blessings Abundant

But before a detailed examination of the covenantal promises, there were basic theological principles to be gleaned from Abram's meeting with the pre-existent Christ. He learned them in silence, but Sheba was probably far from quiet! The profound and searching questions with which Solomon was inundated from his obviously excited and intrigued guest, would undoubtedly have concerned that sublime and exquisite moment in her 'father's' life.

The first lesson was the most obvious one of all, almost too obvious to mention, the realisation that the realm to which the Visitor belonged is altogether Other than the one Abram and Sheba inhabited. The glorious appearance alone would have testified to that, even before a word was spoken. Therefore Abram learned as swiftly as the Stranger's arrival, what Solomon was later to compose and teach Sheba, that the only response to the presence of God is reverence and awe. Where it is absent, so is he: 'for God is in heaven, and thou upon earth, therefore let thy words be few' (Eccles.5:2).

Almighty God is enthroned within his 'holy temple' (Hab.2:20); silence therefore is golden. In practice, it meant that although Abram was an idolater when confronted by his Visitor – and Sheba too, when introduced to Solomon – Abram did not dare 'reply against God' (Rom.9:20), even when commanded to forsake his country, culture and comforts.

Then when the initial shock had abated, to his astonishment it must have dawned upon him that his Visitor had not only arrived uninvited, but knew where he lived! How could that be, unless his name had been known to the Stranger before the visit? And if so, would it not have been referred to in the realm from which the Stranger had come (John 1:48,49)? In fact, as was evident from the unfolding of the covenant, Jehovah the God of glory had not only known Abram's name and where he lived, but had set him apart from everyone else for the task allotted him (Luke 10:20).

To one accustomed to 'wooden' or 'stony' religion, the idol staring impassively into space, the realisation must have been astonishing, even before the truth was understood. The Patriarch's introduction to the 'theophany' had been 'determined' before the first tick of time!

It is remarkable, a great mystery, which Sheba would also have learned from Solomon, that Jehovah's activities are not limited to the framework of time, but are 'from everlasting, from the beginning, or ever the earth was' (Prov.8:23). The true and living God (Jer.10:10) had 'known' Abram and Sheba before the universe was created, had brought them to their mothers' wombs (Jer.1:8), and unknown to them had observed them as they grew to adulthood (Ps.139:1-13), and to the roles for which they were already divinely appointed (Is.44:24); he a prosperous farmer, 'very rich in cattle, in silver, and in gold' (Gen.13:2), and she of royal blood.

Of course, they had been unaware of Who and what lay behind the favours they enjoyed, probably attributing them to their gods, 'good fortune', or in Abram's case, to hard work. But then, how could they whose souls had never penetrated beyond the moon, and who had kept company with idols of wood and stone, have been capable of touching even the hem of the Infinite? Spiritual darkness can produce ideas, mental images, hopes and dreams about the Divine, but never light upon the subject (Is.55:8). But now that light was dawning: upon Abram BEFORE he departed for the Promised Land, and upon Sheba AFTER she had arrived there.

Abram's mysterious Guest knew exactly where he lived, because he it was who had provided him with his home! In fact, everything he owned. Likewise, as Solomon would undoubtedly have taught Sheba in one of their first question-and-answer sessions together, her decision to travel to Jerusalem had not been solely hers. Who did she think had placed the desire in her heart, and drawn her to Solomon (Luke 19:5), reminiscent of his being drawn through the wilderness to his wedding at Zion (Cant.3:6-11)? Solomon's visitor had arrived from 'a far country' (1 Kings 8:41); Abram's, from 'afar' (Ps.139:2).

In other words, Abram and Sheba had been introduced experientially to the truth revealed to every infant in the faith at the 'breast' of the Word (1 Peter 2:2), that to know God is to recognise his sovereign power. He is the Holy One without equal (Is.40:25) tolerating no rivals (Is.42:8), raising up and casting down (Exod. 9:16; Rom.9:17); showing mercy and loving grace, not to everyone (Mal.1:2,3; Rom.9:13), but to his elect (Exod.33:19; Rom.9:15). As Abram learned from the great Teacher himself, 'is anything too hard for the Lord' (Gen.18:14)? Sheba too would have learned from HER teacher the meaning of King David's reference to God's greatness, power, victory and majesty (1 Chron. 29:11). How different was all this from idolatrous worship!

The people of God are invited to seek God following a period of backsliding (Is.55:6; Jer.25:5,6), but mankind's fall from the pleasure and presence of God has paid a terrible price to the souls of those who are not (Gen.2:17). They are spiritually 'dead', not 'unconscious' (Ephes.2:1), unable and unwilling to know, fear, or worship him. Thus, could Abram, or Sheba, have 'found God' (to employ a modern notion) by self-effort? They were as 'dead' to the realm of the Spirit as their idols of wood and stone (Ps.135:18). It was he who 'found' THEM (John 15:16).

Having 'found' Abram (Luke 15:5), the old man was now the first of the privileged covenant people (Gal.3:9), his idols forsaken (1 Thess.1:9) and the almighty God believed to be 'most high' (Gen.14:22). In fact, the 'possessor of heaven and earth' (Matt.11:25). And Solomon's 'high view' of God – too mighty even for the 'heaven of heavens' (1 Kings 8:27) – was passed on to Sheba. As her visit to Jerusalem drew to its close she clearly believed as he did: 'Blessed be the Lord thy God, which delighteth in thee' (1 Kings 10:9).

FROM OBSCURITY TO NATIONHOOD

At a later date, when he was able to reflect objectively upon his momentous experience, Abram would have noted how breathtaking was the scope of the divine purpose. The One whose name would be revealed to Moses as I AM (Exod.3:14; John 8:58), now assured Abram of the future sevenfold blessings with the words 'I WILL: '(1) I WILL make of thee a great nation, and (2) I WILL bless thee, and (3) make thy name great, and thou (4) shalt be a blessing; and I WILL (5) bless them that bless thee, and (6) curse him that curseth thee, and (7) in thee shall all families of the earth be blessed' (Gen.12 :2,3).

Then, a more detailed examination of the remarkable statement would have revealed to Abram how repetitious it is, several words featuring more than once. If the future tense is mentioned six times – 'I will' four of them, and 'shall' on two occasions – two concepts are prominent; greatness (twice), and blessedness (five times), while Abram is referred to in all seven clauses! It was a measure of the gift of faith Abram had received (Ephes.2:8), even at this early stage, that he was not completely overcome to realise his name was pivotal to an understanding of these divine promises. Hence, it was always to be referred to as 'the Abrahamic Covenant'.

GREATNESS

'I WILL make of thee...'; but surely Abram had not heard correctly. A nation, a GREAT nation (Gen.12:2)? He could have been excused his astonishment, and also his bewilderment, as he listened open-mouthed to his Guest. If Abram had been startled by the suddenness of his experience, and taken aback when commanded to prepare for a journey into the unknown (Heb.11:8), this fresh revelation must have caused furrows to cross his brow. Not that he questioned his Visitor, whose authoritative presence made acceptance straightforward, but his thoughts nevertheless must surely have been racing.

A NATION, A GREAT nation, he was to become a GREAT NATION! It took time for the mind to fathom what it had been asked to receive, and in any case, what did it mean? Thoughts of Noah's family, already mentioned, must have sprung to mind yet again. The One who was speaking to him now had once spoken to Noah and his three sons. It was following the trauma of the flood, and an unusual command was given to THEM too, 'Be fruitful, and multiply, and replenish the earth' (Gen.9:1). Needless to say, it was one of history's greatest turning points, with the world divided into three distinct sections. Not just nations arose, but entire races, as stated earlier: Shem and the Semites, Ham and Japheth of the dark and fair skinned peoples respectively (Gen.10:1-5).

In other words, Abram was obviously aware that as something similar had already occurred in history, what he had heard about his own situation could and would be fulfilled. Clearly, through him the world was due to experience another mighty turning point.

A GREAT NATION

However, understandably, the information was puzzling. The only nation, and a great one, Abram knew was the one in which he had lived all his long life – Mesopotamia. In fact, so mighty, it ranked with Egypt as the foci of political and cultural energy for the known world, although, this was not surprising. Egypt's river Nile, and the rivers Euphrates and Tigris of Mesopotamia, assured both powerful nations of commercial prosperity, and therefore of a very wide radius of political influence.

The citizens of Mesopotamia then, not without good reason, were a proud and confident people, privileged and protected, whose lives revolved around worship and water: the worship of Nannar the moon-god, and the waters of the Euphrates and Tigris. The one was prayed to, the others prospered from; the people served the god, and the rivers served the people.

Abram and his contemporaries were only too well aware of what they owed the two great rivers flowing through the nation. These were not merely to be admired, but utilized, and the Mesopotamians were masters of irrigation. Canals and ditches spread the waters across the terrain, of what had once been dry desert, resulting in a luxuriant display: forests, lush green fields, acres of corn and barley, fig trees, and groves of date-palms. One can, therefore, understand how Abram must have felt when called upon to leave such a haven of plenty.

At this point, his thoughts were surely reflected in one of Sheba's questions: HOW would it, how could it, happen? The ages of Noah's sons and daughters-in-law are not known, but they were young enough to produce offspring – but Abram? How could an entire nation materialise from an old man? Centuries later the eighty-year-old Moses was commanded to lead a nation out of Egypt (Acts 7:23,30), the task however required ten miracles to complete (Exod.7-12). But leadership of that kind was not to be Abram's role, nor were many miracles anticipated; just two would prove sufficient to produce a nation. And what mighty miracles they would have to be, in which two very old people were involved (Rom.4:19).

However, what Abram did not know when informed about this miraculous mystery – although Sheba probably did, assuming as one can that this was the area of discussion, it being important enough – was that, to make the remarkable promise even more 'impossible' to fulfil, another twenty five years would elapse before the old couple would experience its fruition! By then, he would be a hundred, and his wife ninety (Gen.12:4; 17:17) But 'is anything too hard for the Lord (Gen.18:14)?' Abram was to discover the answer.

A GREAT NAME

Sheba's quest was to discover the significance of a name, THE 'name' (1 Kings 10:1). Being an intelligent woman, it would have intrigued her still further to realise that before her curiosity could be satisfied another name had first to be discussed; that there is a vital connection between the two. It was the name of her 'father'.

At last! Here was an obvious question to have been asked, which undoubtedly had played upon her lips from the moment Solomon had first touched upon the history of his people. Why did her 'father' possess two names? Solomon had informed her that 'Abraham' had married her 'mother' Keturah (Gen.25:1), yet had spent the rest of the time speaking of 'Abram'! At what point therefore was the name changed? By whom, and why WAS it changed?

Then Solomon would have explained that her 'father', one of Terah's three sons (Gen.11:26), had been named Abram at birth, a name his family assumed was his for life. But the extraordinary appearance of Deity at his side, and the proclamation of the covenant which resulted from it, was the reason why his name was altered. Sheba had to remember clause three of the covenant, 'and make thy NAME great' (Gen.12:2). She was hearing that word 'great' once more.

Following the Visit twenty nine years had elapsed (Gen.12: 4; 17:1), by which time the Promised Land was Abram and Sarai's home, a period not without its significance (Gen.13-16). Sheba's 'father' experienced another Appearance. There had been others between that first meeting and this one, but this was especially noteworthy. It was the moment when 'Abram' gave way to 'Abraham': 'Neither shall thy name any more be called Abram, but thy name shall be Abraham....' The very old man heard the news while lying prostrate before the One who had just announced his arrival with the words, 'I am the Almighty God' (Gen.17:1,5). No other posture would have been adequate (Exod. 34:8).

The words were solemn, more than at any other time during the previous decade and more, as solemn as the Oath which bound the two participants together (Gen.12:1-3). The covenant was about to be ratified: 'I will make my covenant between me and thee...' (Gen.17:2).

But first, there was a stern reminder that such an undertaking involved two parties, and not just one. No doubt, the reason why there had been a lengthy time-span – the briefest of periods as far as heaven is concerned (2 Peter 3:8) – between their first meeting (Gen.12) and this one (Gen.17) was due to the fact that the Patriarch had been closely observed. The unique position he found himself in, together with the responsibility he bore, demanded nothing less. Essentially, he had proved a worthy recipient of such high honour, in that 'he believed in the Lord', who therefore 'counted it to him for righteousness' (Gen.15:6). However, there were less worthy incidents, when faith was slim and half-truths were told (Gen.12:10-20; 16:1-4). Hence, on the day of the covenant's ratification there was a need for a warning, 'walk before me, and be thou perfect' (Gen.17:1); one which is central not only to the Old Covenant (Deut.18:13), but also to the New (Matt.5:48).

Overshadowed by the divine presence as he lay submissively upon the ground, Abraham once more heard the Word and the words of the Almighty God, the Stranger no more. He could not have helped but notice the subtle, but understandable, change in their relationship since their first meeting. It had deepened considerably, he being accounted righteous (Gen.15:6) had seen to that (Rom.5:1; 2 Cor.5:21), and the alteration in his name underlined the fact. Years earlier, the suddenness of what occurred, and the rapidity with which he was transported from idolatrous 'death' to divine Life, had stunned the old man into a frigid silence (Gen.12:1-3). But now, after many 'theophanous' experiences, during which the two had held converse with each other (Gen.15:1-8), Abraham's silence was due to reverential awe alone.

Because the relationship had matured, and certainly Abraham would have been more at ease this time, the covenant was outlined in greater detail. Initially, such had been the shock at the first sight of glory, it appears to be the reason why the purposes of God were presented with brevity. A gush of information, much of which referred to himself, hurtled towards Abraham: all in just three sentences (Gen.12:2,3)!

But now there was more time to dwell upon details, and besides, the revealing of the covenant had reached its second stage. Abraham and his family were at this time already living in the Promised Land (Gen.12:5,6), the Patriarch having 'paced-it-out' (Gen.13:17), and therefore the emphasis now lay upon the remainder of the covenantal promises. There were more surprises in store.

Once again, as years earlier, Abraham could not have but been impressed by the sublime authority behind all that was being stated. The words 'will' and 'shall' again featuring strongly, initially six, but now eleven times (Gen.12:1-3; 17:2-8)! It was, however, the clarifying of the vision that surely amazed Abraham still further.

From the first visitation he understood that from him would miraculously arise 'a great nation', and that remarkably, in him would 'all families of the earth' receive a blessing (Gen.12: 2,3). Now, though, God unfolded to his servant what that meant in practical terms.

First he reminded Abraham of what he had taught the Patriarch. They had been exciting, breathtaking, lessons. Once within the Promised Land Abraham, or Abram as he was then, was invited to look around him, 'northward, and southward, and eastward, and westward'. Mesopotamia, at first sight, was probably more desirable, but Canaan ('an everlasting possession', Gen.17:8) possessed attractions which only faith could see: 'I WILL make thy seed as the dust of the earth, so that if a man can number the dust of the earth, then shall thy seed be numbered' (Gen.13:14-16).

On another occasion, having horizontally inspected his new country, he was commanded by God to look vertically: 'toward heaven, and tell the stars, if thou be able to number them....so shall thy seed be' (Gen.15:5; 22:17). And ironically, to establish the superiority of the land of his adoption over his country of origin, yet another promise was guaranteed: 'Unto thy seed have I given this land, from the river of Egypt (the Nile) unto the great river, THE RIVER EUPHRATES' (Gen.15:18). In other words, the territory between the two would be even greater! Heaven would see to that. So, what had been promised would be a great nation indeed, consisting of myriads of citizens ('I will be their God', Gen.17:8).

The earth is covered in a great deal of dust, the heavens filled with numerous galaxies (Ps.147:4)! Besides, Abraham would have known the meaning of his new name, 'the father of a great multitude', and in any case had just been reminded that God intended to 'multiply' him 'exceedingly' (Gen.17:2).

But now something new was revealed, so far-reaching in its scope, at first Abraham's mind already grappling with a series of astonishing revelations, would not have been capable of imbibing the information. Even after more than a decade of 'theophanic' experiences, and hearing wonderful things about his future, this fresh word from God had not only to be stated, but repeated twice more. Abraham was destined to become the 'father', not just of one GREAT nation, but of 'many nations'. Yes, 'a father of MANY nations have I made thee'. In fact, not only would the citizens of the one nation be multitudinous, but (literally) the citizens of the nations arising from him would be too (Gen.17: 4-6).

And how excited would Sheba have been to learn that from Abraham would kings arise (Gen.17:6), particularly as at that precise moment she was looking at one of them! Moreover, did not the message infer that she herself as a queen, and a 'daughter' of Abraham, was also included (Gen.25:1)? For those, in any generation, with an interest in 'the name of the Lord' the lesson was enthralling.

BLESSEDNESS

Upon first hearing there was one reference in the list of covenantal promises Abraham would have instinctively understood, the meaning of the words 'ALL FAMILIES'. He already knew their identity – the S(h)emitic, Hamitic and Japhethite races (Gen.10:1-5) – but HOW would they be blessed, and WHAT would be the nature of that blessing? As this extraordinary experience was one where faith and trust were called for, he was not told until later. But nevertheless at that first meeting God had promised blessings, in fact the word was mentioned five times (Gen.12:2,3). These were divided into two parts, and encapsulated in the simple phrase, 'I will bless THEE.....and thou shalt BE a blessing' (Gen.12:2).

BLESSINGS TO BE RECEIVED

Abraham now understood the size of the blessings: large indeed! But was there not something else hidden within that word requiring examination? It appeared likely. Such would be the extent of heaven's favour, that this extraordinary God intended not only to bless him, but would bring the judgment of a curse upon anyone who cursed him (Gen.12:3). In other words, God considered him a very special person, worthy of receiving heaven's equally special protection.

Why? Abraham's answer would have been an obvious one, dependent as it was upon the information provided at the time. The answer: because, within the economy of God's purposes, the old man was central to the establishing of one particular 'great nation', other nations too, which collectively would contain multitudes of citizens. And yet he might have puzzled, was there not something of greater significance, which had been kept hidden from him thus far? Why the severity of the judgment upon his enemies? It seemed to imply that the value of what God intended doing through him did not rest solely in nations, and those inhabiting them, but in an aspect of the covenant not yet revealed. What could it possible be?

BLESSINGS TO BE IMPARTED

How privileged he was, how special, how amazed! On the occasion when the covenant was first opened up to him he had been, as already noted, seventy years of age (Gen.12:4), and when it was ratified in his presence ninety nine (Gen.17:1); not the time of life when much more usefulness could be expected, or many more services rendered. Yet, the covenant was brimful with optimism, and the promises filled with references to the future.

Abraham could not have understood what it all meant, he just trusted the Giver of the promises and believed them implicitly (Gen.15:6). He did not know when the 'great nation' would materialise, or the others either, but an intelligent assumption would have connected them with the promised blessing upon the entire world ('all families'). He believed Noah's three sons would not be disappointed (Gen.10:1-5; 12:3); that as the promised flood was worldwide and did indeed DESTROY all but their family (Gen.6:17), so conversely, the promised worldwide BLESSING would be experienced by 'all families' (Gen.12:3). Abraham was in no doubt about this because he had been provided with one of God's greatest gifts, given only to a minority in each generation (Gal.3:9), that of faith (Ephes.2:8; Heb.11:8-11).

THE MISSING LINK

Solomon and Sheba were sitting not far from where Abraham had pitched his tent all those centuries before (Gen.13:3), and during their question-and-answer sessions the wonder of the covenantal promises surely stirred them both, Solomon afresh, and Sheba for probably the first time. After all, the 'great nation' had arrived and its king was in her presence (Gen.17:6). However, she little realised, that in her quest she would learn about an even greater nation to arise from Abraham (Gal.6:15,16).

But there was still some information missing. Within the Old Covenant a certain phrase kept re-occurring, which on the surface appeared to pass unnoticed by the Patriarch. He had been hearing it for years, but had never queried it, although other matters were (Gen.15:2,3,8 etc). How astonished must Sheba have been to learn the missing item of news, and as for Abraham, when at last it was pointed out to him he found it very amusing (Gen.17:17).

FIVE
Domestic Crises

Perhaps Sheba noticed. 'Thy seed'! His 'SEED'? So THAT was the little phrase Abraham had overlooked at the first meeting (Gen.12:7), and even years later after his arrival in the Promised Land (Gen.13:15,16; 15:5,18; 17:7-10). For him to have 'seed', offspring, he must first have fathered a child! Solomon would have been amused at the expression on Sheba's face when he informed her that Sarah, the child's mother, was ninety years old when she gave birth (Gen.17:17; 21:2)!

THE PRINCESS

Any questioning about the name of the Lord would have to feature this aspect of truth, and therefore, there is no doubting Sheba's intense interest in the woman closer to her 'father' Abraham than any other human being. She would surely have been intrigued. As a woman could she have been other than fascinated by news of a pregnant ninety year old; as a queen learning that 'princess' is the meaning of the name Sarah, or as a 'daughter' of Abraham, that Sarah was also his half-sister? They had shared the same father

(Terah), but not the same mother (Gen.20:12), a fact which worked to their advantage on two occasions, when in Egypt (Gen.12:10-13), and again in Gerar (Gen.20). The questioning would have intensified.

She started life in Mesopotamia as Sarai, within a tightly knit community as marrying her half-brother seems to imply, and despite the comforts she enjoyed as the wife of a wealthy man, the barrenness of her womb would have been a great problem to her for more than one reason (Gen.11:29,30; 13:2). As the barren womb in Solomon's kingdom had always signified the absence of divine blessing (Ps.113:9), the same stigma would have applied in Mesopotamia. Sarai could not have been immune from the gossip and the 'knowing' looks, and this situation had lasted throughout her very long life.

Then picturing the sight of her husband, fresh from his startling encounter with his heavenly Visitor, is best left to an intelligent imagination. Surely, as has already been suggested, he bore the radiance of manifested glory as Moses later did (Exod. 34:29). In any case, would he not have appeared in a state of shock? Whichever confronted her, perhaps both, there was no doubting that something remarkably unusual had occurred. But, when her husband was eventually capable of communicating his experience, the first of a series of possible domestic crises presented themselves to her. Suddenly, the covenantal promises were confronted with practical realities.

A CONFLICT OF INTERESTS

Abram had received important information, now he had to impart it. He, and therefore Sarai (for a man and his wife are as one, Gen.2:24), had been commanded to leave the country. Leave the homeland where they had lived throughout their long lives? Yes, pack up everything, and go. Just like that? WHO said? A glorious Stranger, but a stranger all the same, and One she had never met. WHY did they have to leave? Because he said so! Something wonderful was going to happen. WHAT? Well, through her husband a great nation would arise, and the entire earth would be blessed as a result. HOW? Her husband did not know! The Stranger told him!

(In any case, neither would have had any idea of 'the earth' as a concept, Gen.12:3). WHERE were they going? Again, he had no idea (Heb. 11:8)! Sarai would have been excused for looking quizzically at her husband. Also alarmed. She was an obedient wife (1 Peter 3:6), Abram very much the head of their home life (Ephes.5:23), but she was not an inanimate object without feelings and anxieties. She was also a practical woman (Gen.18:12), and his answers to her many queries were so vague.

How active would Sarai's imagination have been. They were a nomadic people accustomed to journeying between familiar watering holes, but not to distant lands. One moment living contentedly and at peace, and the next packing up everything and setting off across the border to a land they had never seen or heard of before – and worst of all, having to leave behind some of their relatives (Gen.12:1). It was asking a great deal of a wife. In any case, Sarai would have considered the logistical problems involved in such a move; the upheaval in the lives of their servants, and the transportation of the livestock. She could not have envisaged the servants and the livestock being excluded, both an integral part of a wealthy nomad's way of life (Gen.12:5).

Then there were the dangers to be faced on the way, and what awaited them when they arrived? They had long since reached the time of life when it was wiser to remain on familiar territory, not venturing forth to the unknown. And would they ever return? Sarai's mind was busy, but in the circumstances, they were understandable queries. At that stage, not having been introduced to her husband's Visitor, she only had Abram's answers to guide her.

Still, her husband had undoubtedly undergone a compelling experience, startling and transforming. The aged Terah, Abram's father, must have thought so too, as did Lot the old man's grandson. In fact, so impressed was Terah by what he had seen of his son, and heard from him, that despite being about two centuries old was prepared to join the travellers; indeed, as head of the family, lead it (Gen.11:31,32).

It said much for Abram's filial respect for his widowed father, that although under God HIS was the appointed leadership of the party, he nevertheless gave preference to the much older man:

'TERAH took Abram his son, and….went forth….to go into the land of Canaan…. (Gen.11:31).'

Thus, on what turned out to be one of history's most important days, a representative group of Terah's large family left the great city of Ur to head towards the unknown: he, Abram, Sarai, and Lot (Gen.11:31). Mules, donkeys or camels, would have been the means of transport for both the travellers and their possessions. Accompanying them, Sarai's assumption being correct, were herdsmen to guard their employers as well as to watch over the livestock, which probably would have been in plentiful supply. It certainly was soon afterwards (Gen.13:2,5,7), so why not when they left Mesopotamia? Is that not what 'all their substance' refers to (Gen.12:5)?

And when they did, impressive was the sight, as slowly the procession moved forward to begin the long trek (Heb.11:6): the lurching camels, the lowing cattle, the bleating sheep, the goading herdsmen – and the pensive travellers. And who was that Stranger leading the way, as promised ('unto a land that I will shew thee', Gen.12:1), or was his unseen presence known only to Abram?

Either way, it was a comfort to the Patriarch on such an undertaking, on such a journey, to be assured that the One whose purposes he was carrying out had also guaranteed a safe passage (Rom.4:21).

THE STOP OVER

Their journey to the land of promise was along a well-trodden route, known since as the Fertile Crescent; a semi circle, it began its sweep at the Persian Gulf, moved towards Mesopotamia's most northern point, west to Syria, through Canaan, and ended far south at Egypt. The centre of civilization at that period, that is until the 5th century BC, commercial traffic flowed to-and-fro across this wide radius. The travelling family, therefore, would not have felt isolated.

As already noted, in the ancient world the travelling time from Babylon to Jerusalem was four months (Ezra 7:9), and had the family not encamped for a period on the way the journey would have taken that long. However, even had they known their destination, they would not have followed that time scale for more than one reason. To begin with, the animals set the pace, and besides, the purposes of God are never in a hurry to be fulfilled.

But there was another reason: Terah's great age (Gen.11:32). It was not only the animals requiring a lengthy rest along the way, but the entire family, particularly its head. Thus, after what must have seemed an age, having traversed the rich and warm Chaldean terrain – probably passing ancient Erech and the ruins of Babel (Gen.11:1-9) – and over a period of unknown duration, the weary procession passed through the fertile valley of Belikh towards a city called Haran ('Charran', Acts 7:4). They did not know it, but they were about halfway to their eventual destination.

They were also still in Mesopotamia, its northwest region, and would have felt at home. The citizens of Ur and Haran shared much in common, primarily the language and the worship of the moon god, referred to by the people of Shem as 'the Baal of Haran'. Also like Ur, Haran was a prosperous city, although small, known in ancient Assyrian documents as 'Harranu', 'the road'. That is, it lay upon the trade route linking two great capitals, Assyria's Neneveh with Syria's Damascus. Haran therefore was a hive of commercial activity.

It must have been just outside the city walls that Terah's exhausted family and employees encamped, livestock and all.
This was not an overnight stay though, or one lasting a few restful days before moving on. It appears to have been years before they did so, about five (Gen. 12:4), during which time the old man Terah died (Gen.11:32; Acts 7:4). It was therefore an opportune moment, no doubt prompted by the divine command (Moses and the Hebrew nation had a similar experience years later, Exod.40 :36), for the Patriarch and his family to move on, and for the long journey to be brought to its conclusion: 'they went forth to go into the land of Canaan, and into the land of Canaan they came (Gen. 12:7).'

A SIGN OF IMPATIENCE

But what about that reference to Abram's 'seed', and his ninety year old pregnant wife? Sheba would have been extremely fascinated by the history relating to her and Solomon, and that of their two peoples (Gen.12:6 – 15:21), but 'hard questions' about 'the name of the Lord' (1 Kings 10:1) would certainly have laid stress upon the divine promises to Abram's posterity. A miracle indeed, that one so old should father a child!

As the years passed (about sixteen) since the original promise had been given ('Unto THY SEED will I give this land', Gen.12:7), although Abram and Sarai's trust in God's word was strong (Rom.4:18-21), their patience was limited and their attitude petulant. They could wait no longer and went ahead with their own plans, Abram confessing to God that as 'thou hast given no seed' he had made his servant Eliezer his heir (Gen.15:2,3), while Sarai on the other hand appears to have surrendered her expectation ('the Lord hath restrained me from bearing', Gen.16:2). She therefore decided to fulfil God's purposes on her own terms, to speed up the process, by having a child but using another woman for the purpose. Her Egyptian maid Hagar was chosen, and Abram was eighty six years of age at the time (Gen.16:1-16).

In other words, in their impatience Abram and Sarai decided to fall back upon contemporary laws and customs. According to the findings of archaeology in the Fertile Crescent, a childless couple frequently adopted a freeborn slave to look after them when they grew old, supervise their funeral arrangements, and inherit their property. Thus, Abram refers to Eliezer as 'one born in my house' (Gen.15:3). Laban and Jacob faced a similar situation, although in this case the element of adoption was missing (Gen.29-31).

Likewise, what Sarai did was according to the custom in patriarchal times, which stipulated that if a wife was barren she had to provide her husband with a female slave for the sole purpose of child-bearing (Gen.16:2-5). The growth and strength of the family heritage was considered a practical necessity, and vital.

But the situation created tension within the home. Hagar, who had given birth to Abram's son, taunted the childless Sarai. In turn she demanded that her maid should leave the household, together with her infant (Gen.16:4-6); an unacceptable action according to common practice at the time. A slave 'wife' and her offspring were to remain secure within the family unit, and the Lord evidently supported this ruling. He met Hagar alone with her child in a desert place, heard her complaint, told her to humbly return to Sarai, and appropriately named the child Ishmael - 'God shall hear' (Gen.16:7-14).

Abram and Sarai had learned the hard way that the purposes of God are unable to be hastened to their fulfilment, Sarai still had well over a decade of frustration to endure before her promised child was born (Gen.17:21,25). In the meanwhile, with Hagar having returned, Sarai was obliged to observe Ishmael's development, and it is best imagined how she felt during that period. She was still childless, and must surely have heard Abram lovingly yearning over Ishmael in prayer: 'O that Ishmael might live before thee!' It must have been an emotionally upsetting period for her to have to endure.

She must also have heard from her husband what his Lord had promised for Hagar's son, that of blessing and fruitfulness: 'twelve princes shall he beget, and I will make him a great nation' (Gen.17: 18,20). Islam is the result of that promise, and today is fulfilling the prophecy : '.....a wild man, his hand will be against every man, and every man's hand against him, and he shall dwell in the presence of all his brethren' (Gen.16:12).

ANOTHER SURPRISE FOR ABRAHAM

It surely encouraged Hagar during this period of distress, a reminder she had not been overlooked, but God chose to inform his servant that his wife's name would also be changed. Abram had already given way to Abraham, and now Sarai was to be substituted by 'Sarah' ('Princess'), a process signifying heaven's blessing (Gen.17:5,15; Matt.16:17,18; Acts 13:9).

If Abraham responded to the honour just granted to his wife it is not recorded, but at the time his thoughts and prayers were towards his son Ishmael and no doubt the boy's mother (Gen.17: 18). After all, did not the future belong to THEM? Ishmael was only a teenager (Gen.17:25), and therefore Hagar would still have been a young woman (Gal.4:22-26).

The Patriarch and his wife, both of very great age (Gen.17: 17), were at the winter of their lives. The end was surely near. The future belongs to the young! Abraham's thinking was practical, and understandable, but God's thoughts differed from his, and were 'higher' (Is.55:8).

Abraham heard the words, 'I will bless her', and then the astonishing statement that he would father a child by Sarah (Gen.17:16). SARAH? Had he heard correctly? Surely not! Another child from HAGAR, the younger woman, but after all these years of barrenness Sarah was to become PREGNANT? God possesses many surprises! Far from having to submit to the inevitability of old age and therefore to give preference to the younger woman, Sarah had not been overlooked after all.

Abraham's reaction to the extraordinary news was equally extraordinary, particularly as he was in the presence of the Lord, who had not long before addressed him in very solemn tones: 'I am the Almighty God, walk before me, and be thou perfect (Gen. 17: 1).' The Patriarch burst out laughing, but in such a way as to avoid eye contact. Shortly before, upon the Lord's appearance, he had fallen to the ground in a submissive attitude of profound reverence and adoration as Moses did many years later (Exod.34: 8), but now his prostrate posture sought to conceal mirth (Gen.17: 3,17).

And as if God was incapable of hearing his thoughts, even 'afar off' (Ps.139:2), Abraham secretly questioned what he had just been told: 'Shall a child be born unto him that is an hundred years old? And shall Sarah, that is ninety years old, bear?' Then, in place of rejoicing over the wonderful news, Abraham revealed where his heart actually lay in prayerfully expressing his yearning that 'ISHMAEL might live before thee' (Gen.17:17,18).

But God persisted. Ishmael would not be forgotten, in fact would be the recipient of his favour, twelve princes and 'a great nation' arising from him (Gen.17:20), but it was to be from old Sarah's womb that the promised 'seed' would appear. Isaac would be his name, one chosen by God himself, and to him would the covenant made to Abraham be ratified (Gen.17:19).

Then after twenty nine years or so of waiting, for the Patriarch had been about seventy when the Lord first appeared to him (Gen.12:4), at last was revealed when this child of promise would be born: 'the next year' (Gen.17:21).

A SIGN OF THE COVENANT

But something else was revealed that day to Abraham, a piece of information so unusual it may have proved shocking to him. Thus far 'the everlasting covenant' with which he was by this time so familiar, had been conveyed to him by his Lord verbally, with Abraham receiving and believing them as a dutiful listener. But now, after years of listening, it was his turn to signify his acceptance of the covenant by acting upon it. How easy to listen, but much harder is it to 'sign' the agreement with one's own blood!

How Abraham reacted upon initially hearing the general command is unknown - 'Every man child among you shall be circumcised' - probably calmly, because HE was not a child! But then, the divine finger pointed at him personally. Abraham was included! He also was being commanded to be circumcised, and to perform the deed himself (Gen.17:10,11)! Could any man have refrained from flinching?

But what of Sarah and Hagar, and also Sheba when she heard the account from Solomon? How did they react? How did Sarah feel when told by her husband what he intended to do, and then suddenly one day hearing him order every male in his household to undergo the same sensitive operation? Even had they remained silent, although in the circumstances it would have been difficult, when the thirteen year old Ishmael was set aside for the treatment, what drama must have taken place within the family unit (Gen.17:23-25; Acts 7:8).

It would have been hard enough for the men to endure – and Abraham was ninety-nine years old at the time – but how would the teenage Ishmael have coped with the situation? With great difficulty one suspects. And what emotions would have arisen within Sarah, and particularly the boy's mother? Years later, it proved too much for Moses' wife Zipporah. Having performed the act of circumcision upon her own son, which is more than Hagar was obliged to do (Gen.17:23), she raged at Moses, 'Surely, a bloody husband art thou to me' (Exod.4:25). Hearing the account could not have been pleasant for Sheba.

SARAH RECEIVES SOME SURPRISES

Shortly afterwards, as Abraham was sitting outside his tent he was approached by visitors. Sheba would have been intrigued by the Scripture text, which records that 'the Lord appeared', and yet when the old Patriarch glanced up he saw 'three men' standing in front of him (Gen.18:1,2). He quickly recognized the former, his Friend with whom he had had much to do during the previous thirty years (James 2:23), but who were the other two? At one stage, although Abraham addresses the Lord, the two mysterious visitors make their own contribution to the conversation, clearly revealing their authority (Gen.18:3-12). Angels! Later, they made their way to Sodom, leaving their Lord and Master (Heb.1:4) in conversation with Abraham (Gen.18:22; 19:1).

Sarah little realised that day what surprises were in store for her (Gen.18:1-15). For about three decades she had heard her husband tell of his astonishing experiences, of meeting with the Lord and of the remarkable revelations he had received, but all that time she had remained in the background. Now, from inside the tent she heard voices, and soon Abraham appeared and asked her to prepare food for their three guests. It says a great deal for her graciousness as a hostess and her expertise as a cook (as well as her patience!), that a splendid meal was prepared as 'quickly' as her husband had commanded (1 Peter 3:6).

It was during the meal, which the three guests shared together outside the tent with Abraham standing nearby, that Sarah received her first surprise. As her husband had served the visitors, it is to be presumed she had not seen them, but remained within the tent. Nevertheless, she heard the conversation, including the mention of her name as the visitors asked after her whereabouts (Gen.18:8,9). Did Sheba comment upon how strange was this request? There is no way of knowing, but as an intelligent woman she may have been puzzled. He, the second Person of the Trinity, who had introduced himself as 'Almighty God' (Gen.17:1) and who was shortly after to ask rhetorically 'Is anything too hard for the Lord?' (Gen.18:14), appeared not to know where Sarah was; the 'God of glory' (Acts 7:2), and his two angel companions, dependent upon Abraham telling them! It was extremely unlikely.

Of course, they knew where Sarah was, but equally they wanted her to listen. Thus, the importance lay not in the question – 'Where is SARAH thy wife?' (Gen.18:9) - but in the mentioning of her name. From inside the tent she stopped what she had been doing, and listened. How carefully we do so when our names are mentioned, especially when supposedly beyond our hearing, although what is heard is not always to our liking!

It was a most unusual situation. One of the most vital messages known to man was about to be heralded, that saving grace would be channelled historically through Abraham and his wife, and the person it most affected was not actually present to hear it. The Lord had already told Abraham earlier about Sarah's impending pregnancy (Gen.17:19), and therefore the angels knew, but Sarah had yet to receive the shock of her long life.

From the tent door, just out of sight, she continued to listen, and what one of the guests said must surely have astonished her, as well as Sheba upon hearing the account from Solomon. Mysterious words: 'I will certainly return unto thee according to the time of life; and lo, Sarah thy wife shall have a son (Gen.18:10).' But Sarah appears to have overlooked the most significant aspect of the message, apparently hearing (understandably so) only that which concerned her; namely, 'ME, have a child? At my age? Surely not!' Her reaction would have been expected in the circumstances, and was the same as Abraham's. She laughed within herself at the thought (Gen.17:17; 18:12).

Perhaps Sheba, with the benefit of hindsight, picked up on what Sarah had missed as one of her 'hard questions' (1 Kings 10:1). The realm of the miraculous was very evident on that remarkable day, and not only in the announcement of Sarah's forthcoming pregnancy. Clearly, it had been God the Son ('the Lord') who had delivered the message – a miracle in itself – which he introduced with the words 'I WILL', 'CERTAINLY', and 'SHALL' (Gen.18:10). Abraham would have recognised the sovereign authority behind the words, as well as the voice of the LIVING God, reminiscent of that first meeting long before, when the words 'I will' featured so prominently (Gen.12:1-3), and he would have remembered how strange they had appeared to him after a lifetime serving 'DEAD' idols.

But how was the message introduced, which Sarah had apparently overlooked? The tone was serious, the promise decisive, that their mysterious chief Guest would definitely ('I WILL') without doubt ('CERTAINLY') return to Abraham and his wife 'according to the time of life (Gen. 18:10).' The pregnancy then was dependent upon the second Person within the Godhead returning to the couple, but why? The answer was surely because his was the plan and purpose behind it, and therefore the creative and miraculous power to bring it to pass. It was not surprising. Is he not 'the image of the invisible God', and the Creator of 'all things' (Col.1:15,16)?

But Sarah received another surprise, an embarrassment too. At the prospect of having a child at her advanced years she had laughed, silently and secretly. How astonished therefore she must have been to hear the Guest ask her husband why she had done so (Gen.18:13). She was alarmed. How did he know she had laughed, when he could not see her, and in any case, when her amusement had been 'deep down' (Gen.18:12)? Centuries later others were also amazed, when that same Person had known the thoughts of men who had muttered 'within themselves' (Matt.9:3,4). But then, does not almighty God read thoughts from afar (Ps.139:2)?

It would appear that at this point Sarah joined the others outside. It was her first encounter with her husband's heavenly Visitor of thirty years before (Gen.12:1-3). She had heard so much about him, and of the promises made to her husband, and had seen the effect upon him as a result of their many mysterious encounters. Small wonder she was afraid (Gen.18:15).

Yet, not too fearful of speaking to him! How different were the reactions of husband and wife to their first meeting with 'the God of glory' (Acts 7:2)! Abraham was silent throughout that initial encounter when the covenant was established (Gen,12:1-3), so overcome was he and justifiably humbled. The Lord had approached Abraham, but now Sarah was approaching the Lord; Abraham had not spoken a word, too shocked to say anything, but Sarah opened the conversation – and with a lie! She was adamant, she had NOT laughed, but the apostle Peter's words were of course unknown to Sarah: 'thou knowest all things (John 21:17).' His response was immediate, she HAD laughed, and Sarah's embarrassment must have been acute. It has to be an extremely uncomfortable moment confronting eternal Truth with a lie, ultimate Reality with make-belief.

But as promised, Sarah gave birth to Isaac, and he was circumcised by his father on the eighth day as God had commanded (Gen.21:1-5). Years passed, how many can only be guessed at, when Abraham received his greatest shock. So shocking, in fact, one can understand why this fresh incident was kept on hold for over thirty years, because before this period the Lord had not even hinted what he intended doing.

The moment began very simply, Abraham clearly having no notion of what was to follow. Unlike that first occasion, when the Lord had suddenly appeared unannounced (Gen.12:1), this time he called the old Patriarch by name. Abraham responded cheerily, 'Behold, here I am (Gen.22:1).' Then it happened.

SIX
The Greatest Crisis

Of all the domestic crises Abraham and Sarah faced together over those many years, this undoubtedly was the most traumatic. They had experienced personal encounters with the great God; the transformation from gross idolatry to saving faith; the forsaking of their culture and creature comforts; the emotional farewells to relatives and friends; the crossing over from the old country to the new; the births of Hagar's child Ishmael and Isaac the child of promise; the initial trauma that circumcision would have caused, and the drama behind the banishing of Hagar and Ishmael from Abraham's house at Sarah's request (Gen.21:9-12). Now this.

Once again, as at the first, the Lord did not gradually and gently lead into the theme of his visit (Gen.12:1). There were no hints of what was to follow. On the contrary, the command was direct; not a word too many. Sheba must have wondered how expressive were Abraham's feelings when he heard the Lord's message: 'Take now thy son, thine only son Isaac, whom thou lovest, and get thee into the land of Moriah, and offer him there for a burnt offering upon one of the mountains which I will tell thee of (Gen.22:2).' Just that!

The text is silent about Abraham's reaction to what he had just heard. True, he was a great man of faith, and a faithful man, but not a machine. He had just been told to kill his son! No amount of faith in God and devoted obedience to him could possibly smother deep-rooted paternal instincts. It was one of the most dramatic of all moments.

A PROFOUND CONFLICT

Isaac, to be killed: killed? Killed, and HE had to do it! Kill his son, and in cold blood. Murder, when God himself had forbidden it (Gen.9:6)! True, it was to be a religious act, but it amounted to the same thing. Abraham's dark thoughts are best imagined as they chased each other around his mind, and what blackened them still further, would have been the realisation of the many hours that were to be spent anticipating the deed. The land of Moriah (a summit of a range of hills later called Mount Zion, Ps.2: 6) was many miles away, at least three days' journey (Gen.22:4), and throughout that period he would be wrestling with these conflicting emotions.

But if Solomon told Sheba this story – and it is important enough in her quest for him to have done so – would she not have discovered something in the account that would have softened the Patriarch's stress? Could it not be argued that he believed, either by faith or revelation from God, that Isaac would survive? Either that, or if killed would be miraculously raised from the dead? In the story there are two moments which appear to argue in favour of that being so (Gen.22:5,8).

Then, as Abraham pondered the situation, Sarah would spring to mind. She would have to be told. How would he put it to her; that he was going to kill their son? Of course, he would not, could not, confront her with such a bold statement. Sarah had laughed when she heard that she would give birth to Isaac (Gen.18: 13), but he could imagine her reaction now to the news of his impending demise. In seeking to make the issue more acceptable to her therefore he would sweeten the pill, speak of it in pious terms, by referring to the question of their precious son being offered to God. But, to a mother that still sounded like killing him!

The thought also surely passed through Abraham's mind that he would not tell Sarah, except to say that he and Isaac had been commanded by God to go on a journey together. They would be away over a week (Gen.22:4). If Abraham, by faith or revelation, believed Isaac would return with him then all would be well. After a week or two they would be back and Sarah would be none the wiser, or would she be? What about the curiosity factor? WHERE were they going, and WHY, and WHAT did they intend doing when they got there?

But supposing he did NOT know Isaac would return, what then? How could he tell Sarah that he and Isaac were going away, but only one of them would be returning home? Perhaps, it would be best if he and Isaac just left surreptitiously, without telling her, but no, that was out of the question. If Isaac was to die, how dreadful that he was not given an opportunity to see his mother before he went on his fateful journey. In any case, Sarah's surprise at their sudden departure would swiftly turn to shock when Abraham returned home alone. What a complicated affair it was!

But there was still Isaac to consider. His age at the time is unknown. He was young enough to have been unmarried (Gen. 24:4), and in any case, Abraham referred to him as a 'lad' (Gen. 22:5). Whatever his age, though, the actual reason for his being taken to the land of Moriah was understandably kept hidden from him. He believed the worship of God was the reason, and that the sacrificial lamb for the burnt offering would be discovered when they arrived at the scene (Gen.22:5,8).

It would appear that is what Sarah had also been told, because knowing her son was soon to die, how could she have kept her emotions under control when she bade him farewell at the start of the journey, and thus creating suspicion in Isaac's mind? It could not have been done. Instead, she was content to watch father and son depart, believing she would see them again in a week or so (Gen.22:4).

Early on the day of the departure there was much activity, an ass to be saddled and wood for the burnt offering collected and strapped to the animal, and no doubt farewells to be made. Abraham, Isaac and two employees were then ready to set off on what for the father and the son was to be an astonishing journey of discovery.

THOUGHTS ALONG THE WAY

The little party slowly made its way from the homestead at Beer-sheba – and Sheba would have been fascinated by the name, and by the fact that it was the most southern tip of Solomon's kingdom (Gen.21:22-33; 1 Kings 4:25) – towards mount Moriah just under forty five miles away in the north west.

Halfway there they would have passed through Mamre, or Hebron as it was later called, the town that Sheba would have heard much about from Solomon. In that town Abraham and Sarah were eventually buried (Gen.23:19; 25:8,9), and it was at Hebron David reigned for seven years, and where six of his children were born (1 Kings 2:11; 1 Chron.3:1-4).

Throughout the tiring journey the old Patriarch, sitting astride the only means of transport the four possessed, had much to think about (Gen.22:3). Isaac might have been leading the way, holding the animal's reins, or walking alongside his father so there was only one topic that could occupy his mind. As one mile succeeded another, the land of Moriah getting ever closer, Abraham must have analysed the message he had received (Gen. 22:2).

The second part of it was all too clear. His son was to be offered up as a burnt sacrifice, but did he understand the significance of the first half of the message, 'Take now thy son, thine only son Isaac, whom thou lovest'? Moses the inspired author under God, appears to have done so, in which case, why not Abraham to whom the Lord provided mighty revelations?

To Moses had been revealed the foundation upon which all the messianic promises of the Old Testament dispensation were laid, namely, that declaration made in Eden to the serpent: 'I will put enmity between thee and the woman, and between thy seed and her seed; it shall bruise thy head, and thou shalt bruise his heel (Gen.3:15)'. It is a messianic statement of vital importance; a statement which strongly hints, not only at the eventual arrival of a Messiah to wage war against Satan, but also of his victory over the enemy of souls even if in the process the Victor would be 'bruised' (Is.53:5).

As a consequence, when the Lord in his meetings with Abraham had been repeatedly referring to his 'seed' (Gen.12:7; 13:15; 15:5 etc), would not the old man have associated the reference to God's declaration in Eden ('between thy seed and her seed')? It seems likely. In which case, would not Abraham have also noted the significance of the reference to his 'ONLY SON Isaac, whom thou LOVEST'? It seems inconceivable, that having encountered the pre-existent Christ he would have remained ignorant of the relationship between the Father and the Son.

If that were so, then Abraham must have understood what is now known as the Gospel, that he and Isaac – although was his son an unwitting participant? – were involved in a spiritually dramatic parable. Why did God command that the Patriarch's beloved and 'only son' Isaac must be offered as a burnt offering (Gen.22:2), unless it was a reminder that heaven in some unique way would share the experience; that it would foreshadow a sacrifice of another 'only Son', beloved of his Father (Matt.17:5)? Or again, was it just a coincidence, or the result of a revelatory experience, that caused the father in taking the wood for the burnt offering to lay it upon his son (Gen.22:6), foreshadowing a greater event when the Son carried some wood given him by the Father on his way to make the ultimate Sacrifice (John 19:17)?

WISDOM IMPARTED

And what of Solomon? Did HE understand the foundational prophecy as recorded by Moses (Gen.3:15), and the parable that lay behind the Lord's reference to Abraham's beloved 'only son' (Gen.22:2)? It is more than likely he did, and therefore these great truths featured in Sheba's quest.

As she sat in a luxurious house at the King's feet, being transported from the mundane to the marvellous, she was not to know of another lady who far beyond her days would be seated in a lowly house at the feet of the King of all kings. Both women listened intently to 'that good part, which shall not be taken away' from them (Luke

10:42), Mary to the Son of David, and Sheba to David's son; Truth speaking to Mary of heavenly matters (John 14:6; 18:37); Wisdom revealing 'excellent things' to Sheba (Prov. 8:6,7).

No better 'part' could there be than that which related to the Messiah, his relationship to heaven, and his unique ministry at the behest of God; the two ladies therefore would have been led through three stages by their respective teachers. First Sheba, under Solomon's tutelage, grappled with the mysterious concept of 'Wisdom', Mary through Jesus with that of 'the Word'. As she learned that the Word was from 'the beginning', and indeed 'was God' (John 1:1), Sheba understood that 'in the beginning' was Wisdom (Prov.8:22); that Wisdom was 'set up from everlasting' (Prov.8:23). If the Word then 'was God', so too is Wisdom.

At the same time, Mary would have discovered that the Word was not only God, but was also 'with God' (John 1:1); the everlasting Father and the Prince of Peace identified with each other within the Godhead (Is.9:6). The 'Prince' is 'one' with the Father (John 10:30), and in seeing him, the Father has also been 'seen': 'I am in the Father, and the Father in me' (John 14:9-11). To believe in the Father therefore demands belief in the Son, to 'know' the one is to 'know' the other (John 17:5; 14:1). Sheba likewise heard Solomon's version of the same truths. Wisdom, 'possessed' by 'the Lord', was 'always' his 'delight', in fact during the creation was 'by him, as one brought up with him' (Prov.8:22-32).

Finally, although Sheba lacked the advantage of having the Word 'made flesh' (John 1:14) seated beside her (Luke 10:39), she nevertheless learned the truth from two different sources. First was Solomon. His casket of mysteries contained more truth than Sheba could have imagined. Not only had he been gifted with revelatory experiences, as his written works convey, but he had also inherited the truth of the Gospel his father had received and committed to parchment. He, 'the sweet psalmist of Israel' (2 Sam.23:1), would have taught his son from an early age, and this was Sheba's second avenue of discovery.

David had 'heard' that 'moment' in eternity when a covenant was made between the Father and the Son to secure the redemption of the elect: the Father expressing his eternal love and 'delight' in the Son (Prov.8:30) - 'Thou art my Son, this day have I begotten thee. Ask of me....' (Ps.2:7,8) - whose reciprocation was similarly expressed in a sacrificial commitment, 'Lo, I come....I delight to do thy will, O my God....' (Ps.40:7,8; John 8:29).

But David not only 'heard', he was also enabled to 'see'. Presciently, he 'witnessed' the Messiah's anguish as well as his glory: his alienated family (Ps.69:8; John 7:3-8), his contemptuous contemporaries (Ps.22:7,8; 69:9), his tormented death (Ps.22:1-21), his remarkable resurrection (Ps.16:8-11), his triumphant ascension (Ps.110:1), and the establishing of his eternal throne and kingdom (2 Sam.7:13,16).

Sheba learned all this. Would Solomon have refrained from telling her, anymore than Jesus could have withheld the truth from Mary? Sheba also understood, that to discover Wisdom is to find 'life', and conversely, to reject and hate him is to harm's one's soul – and 'die' (Prov.8:35,36). Equally, Mary heard One greater than Solomon declare (Matt.12:42), that to know Truth is also to discover Life (John 14:6) and liberation (John 8:32); to ultimately reject him is to die in one's sins (John 8:24).

FOUR CURIOUS EYES!

At last, after three days, their destination was in sight albeit 'afar off' (Gen.22:4). It must have been an exhausting journey, particularly for the aged Abraham, who clambered down from the ass and gave instructions to his two employees to remain where they were to look after the animal while he and his son went off to worship.

How curious the young men would have been to know what was going on! As employees they had obviously been kept in the dark about what would take place at Moriah, and for three days were kept wondering why they had been instructed to make such a journey. Now, they were being told the reason. They might not have minded so much had they been supplied with an animal to ride upon, but instead, they had walked for three tiring days – and then they learn it was so that the old man and his son could worship (Gen.22:5)! Could they not have worshipped back home? Why travel for three days to do it? And when their employer and his son returned, from wherever they were going, they had another three days of walking to undertake. The two men could not have been pleased.

Curious eyes watched Abraham strap wood upon his son's back, and produce a knife and the means for lighting a fire (Gen. 22:6), before the two walked off into the distance. To the watching men they appeared an odd couple, the very old man and the youth, the latter laden with wood and the former with thoughts. And how strange, that in his frailty their employer had required transport for the three days journey, but was now prepared to walk to his destination 'afar off'. Clearly, he did not want his two employees to observe the act of 'worship' (Gen.22:4,5). It was a mystery, which in turn would have stimulated their curiosity still further.

But unknown to the young men Abraham had left behind him another mystery, in what on the surface appeared a very ordinary statement, his final instruction to them: 'I and the lad will go yonder and worship, AND COME AGAIN TO YOU' (Gen.22: 5). It was a seemingly casual remark, but Abraham held the truth that lay behind it close to his chest. He had been commanded to offer Isaac as a burnt offering (Gen.22:2), and killing his son was the only way he could it, and yet he assured his two employees that he and Isaac would return to meet them again. Had they realised they were being introduced to the most glorious good news history could receive, that following the ultimate Sacrifice a resurrection would occur (Matt.16:21), Abraham's servants would possibly not have been so impatient to return home!

A PERTINENT QUESTION

Not only Abraham's mind was filled with thoughts, but Isaac's too. How long the two had been walking is unknown, but a great intelligence was not required to cause Isaac to be puzzled. Perhaps throughout the long journey, and now even more so, missing elements in the equation had occupied his thinking.

Like the two men he had just left behind, Isaac must have considered it unusual to travel so far from home to worship. In any case, as he had to carry all the wood on his back, he of all people was entitled to wonder why the animal could not have been used for that purpose. His father's employees probably had thought the same, but guessed being ordered to look after the ass was a ploy to keep them rooted to the spot (Gen.22:5).

Then again, Isaac knew the offering of a sacrifice demanded a lamb as the victim, but his father had brought everything with him, except the most important item. Pertinent questions circulated Isaac's mind, but only one was audible.

The situation was not only unusual, but also very strange, and the way he opened up the conversation appears to reveal his bewilderment. Just two words were spoken, that is all, clearly arising after a great deal of thought since they left home, 'My father' (Gen.22:7), because it does not take three days to notice two objects out of the three. He had the wood (no doubt getting heavier with each step), and his father the means for lighting the fire, but the equation was incomplete. The victim: where was the lamb (Gen.22:7)?

Abraham's reply was matter-of-fact, 'God will provide himself a lamb for a burnt offering', and it satisfied Isaac's curiosity. No more questions were forthcoming, no further comment, 'so they went both of them together' (Gen.22:8). But, brief though his father's response had been, Isaac was unaware that behind it lurked the possibility of it being interpreted in several different ways. The first can be discounted – 'There'll be no problem getting a lamb' - that believing his son was going to die, Abraham deliberately lied to him. It has already been ascertained, that even if Isaac remained ignorant, Abraham understood the significance of what was happening.

Then there is the more sinister and cynical interpretation – 'God will supply a lamb alright; you are it!' – but this too has no basis in truth on account of what is known about the Patriarch's character and experience of God. In any case, had Abraham anticipated Isaac's death the expression on his face would have revealed that something unwelcome was at hand, but Isaac appeared fully satisfied with his father's reply and did not question further.

In fact, the words 'God will provide himself a lamb' is an heroic expression of steadfast faith, not only in Abraham's grasp of this

Gospel parable in which he and Isaac were involved, but particularly of his belief in the trustworthiness of Almighty God's righteousness (Gen.15:6; 17:1). Abraham was not clairvoyant, he was unable to 'see' the actual details of what would happen on Mount Moriah, except that he knew he would be caught up in an unique emotional conflict.

However, God's gift of faith (Ephes.2:8) had provided him with 'sight' of another kind. As he drew nearer to the appointed venue, faith could 'see' there was no question of the event being cancelled, God's Word being unalterable and inerrant. Faith also 'saw' the altar with the sacrificial offering lying upon it; 'witnessed' the kindness of the Patriarch's Friend (2 Chron.20:7) in supplying a substitute (James 2:23), for that act was an essential aspect of the parable being enacted (2 Cor.5:21); 'observed' his beloved 'only son' Isaac returning home with him (Gen.22:2,5; Matt.17:5). Truly, 'all things work together for good to them that love God, to them who are the called according to his purpose' (Rom.8: 28).

FAITH FULLY STRETCHED

At last the walk was over, the old man and his son only too pleased to have arrived; Abraham because of his advanced age, and Isaac desirous of removing the heavy load from his back. No doubt the three days journey, followed by the lengthy trudge to the Mount (Gen.22:4), had taken their toll.

It is not recorded but presumably they rested, although it would not have been for long as there were important things to do. Soon, Abraham was on his feet and began building the altar. Sheba might have wondered why that task was left to the very old man, beyond his centenary, when Isaac was available to perform the heavy work. The answer lay in the fact that there was much more to erecting an altar than at first might seem to be the case. At a later date, God's commands and instructions were committed to writing (Exod.20:24-26), but Abraham with his experiences of meeting with God would have been conversant with them.

Much care had to be taken. This was not an altar dedicated to a pagan deity, with 'eyes' incapable of seeing (Ps.115:5) the antics being performed in its name (1 Kings 18:26), but rather a solemn venue where the wrath of a sin-hating God was appeased and man's sin was 'covered', as Solomon's father so aptly put it (Ps.32: 1,2); where mercy and truth met, and where righteousness and peace embraced each other (Ps.85:10). Therefore more was required in the design and structure of the altar than the zeal of a strong man.

The first consideration was to achieve the correct order of priorities. Sinful man would emphasise sight rather than faith, the altar he could see and not the being of the invisible God: how magnificent would be that altar, how decorative! But the almighty God demanded a lowly altar, befitting the state of man in constant need of mercy and forgiveness. It would be constructed of earth, reminding man of his lowly origins (Gen.2:7), or of stone (1 Kings 18:32) directing his thoughts to God the Rock (Ps.18:2), but on no account was the altar to be ornate or with steps leading to it as in pagan worship (Exod.20:24-26).

Abraham had constructed many altars, but none like this, when his solemn task was undertaken with such a heavy heart. Was he capable of speaking to Isaac? Surely, the only sound that could be heard would be that of the old man breathing heavily as he performed his duty. Isaac stood watching, unaware of how intense was the drama being enacted on the mount at that moment; the emotional conflict within his father. He must have sensed all was not well, as he glanced around in search of a lamb (Gen.22:7).

The work having been completed there was just one simple task left for Abraham to do, which in the circumstances he must have wished would take him longer, because when finished the climax of the three days drama would have been reached. His heart beat faster as he picked up the wood that Isaac had carried to the spot, and with meticulous care laid it 'in order' upon the altar (Gen.22:9), each piece placed with care in such a way the flames would be encouraged to roar heavenward (Lev.1:12). Just think, his own son could be enveloped in those flames!

THE KNIFE POISED

The moment had arrived, all too soon. Abraham placed the final piece of wood into position, and then looked at Isaac. The altar was now ready for use, and his beloved 'only son' stood nearby ready to fill it (Gen.22:2). Years before the Patriarch had made an impassioned and heart-rending plea to God: 'O that ISHMAEL might live before thee! (Gen.17:18)'; how deeper must the anguish have been at this crucial moment, 'O that ISAAC might live....'.

But what was Isaac thinking in that instance? For three days he had walked with his father, could not have helped noticing how thoughtful he was, and now on Mount Moriah how strained was the silence. There were so many unanswered questions: why the long journey, what secret was his father hiding, what was it all about? Then he saw the old man slowly walking towards him, with what must have been an unusual expression on his face, prompting yet another question: what was his father up to? Isaac stood rooted to the spot as his father came within an arm's distance.

Suddenly, Abraham grabbed the unsuspecting 'lad' and in the struggle that ensued managed to bind him, until he was captive at the hands of his gasping father (Gen.22:5,9). The astonished Isaac must have cried out in the skirmish protesting at the apparent madness of what was happening. His father must have lost his senses! What was he doing?

He very quickly discovered, as he was dragged (surely the old man could not have carried him) towards the altar. Once there, Abraham heaved his son from the ground onto it, and then pushed and shoved him into position on the wood. All this time, in a panic, Isaac would have been appealing to his father to think again at what he was doing, but there was no respite in the Patriarch's endeavour to sacrifice his son in obedience to God's command and purpose.

Isaac lay helpless at his father's mercy, nevertheless still pleading for it, watching his father reach for the sharp knife. It was now in his hand. Breathing heavily, with sweat on his brow and prayers on his lips, Abraham raised his arm the knife glistening in the sunlight ready to plunge it into his only son, whom he loved (Gen.22:2). There it hovered menacingly for several seconds, but to Isaac it seemed many minutes ...

But is that what happened? A superficial glance at the text gives that appearance: Abraham 'laid the wood in order, and bound Isaac his son, and laid him on the altar upon the wood' (Gen.22:9). But the day was filled with mysteries, and one manifested itself between the laying of the wood and the binding of Isaac.

Certainly, when the wood had been laid Abraham must have looked at Isaac, but what then? The old Patriarch was very old indeed, well over one hundred, and Isaac a strong young man: had not his father referred to him as a 'lad', and was it not he who had been sturdy enough to carry the wood on his back for all those miles (Gen.22:5,6)? In which case, could Sheba imagine Abraham being capable of binding a struggling Isaac, dragging him to the altar and then heaving him onto it? The effort would have killed him.

And once the significance of this remarkable occasion on Mount Moriah had been explained to her by Solomon – and the location of the glorious temple in Jerusalem would have undoubtedly produced answers to her many questions (2 Chron. 3:1) – Sheba realised that not only practically, but also theologically, there is something awry about the above scenario. In it, Isaac is presented as being ignorant of the parable being enacted, but for it to be fully expressed, both father and son would have to grasp its significance, and not just one of them.

Was the Father's beloved 'only Son' unaware of his mission and commission; that even when he arrived at the 'altar' of Sacrifice at Calvary, under the weight of wood, he had no idea what was happening, and was forced to die against his wishes? Such a notion would not only disqualify the account as one of spiritual significance, but much more to the point, the Messiah's Gospel would cease to have relevance. So, what ACTUALLY occurred at that extraordinary moment when the altar was completed?

The answer may lie further back in time, when Isaac's curiosity got the better of him, and his father replied: 'My son, God will provide himself a lamb for the burnt offering', and then, 'they went both of them together' (Gen.22:8). The question having been posed, was that not the opportunity required for Abraham to introduce Isaac to the parable, and his involvement in it? If so, then one can understand why they had such a long walk to Moriah, it being 'afar off', and why the two servants were not permitted to get closer to the mount (Gen.22:4,5). Abraham and his son had a great deal to discuss, in an emotionally charged atmosphere.

If this assumption is correct, by the time Isaac arrived at the mount he had already made the necessary commitment to God and to his father, in an extraordinary act of faith and courage: 'I do always those things that please him' (John 8:29). The father Abraham 'gave' his only son (John 3:16); Isaac the son warmly responded, 'I delight to do thy will' (Ps.40:8). If this is what occurred, as seems likely, it reveals Isaac as a great man of faith like his father, and places him in a heroic mould. Small wonder the covenant made to Abraham (Gen.12:1-3) was ratified to his son (Gen.26:24,25).

So, the old man with twine in his hands did not need to approach the 'lad' after all, because it was not a struggling Isaac he bound, but a submissive young man. As the father waited by the altar, the son walked to it – 'I CAME....not to do mine own will, but the will of him that sent me' (John 8:38) – and permitted his father to bind him, who having done so, gently laid him upon the wood-covered altar (Gen.22:9).

In her quest, Sheba would have learned that Isaac was a 'type' of the promised Seed, the Messiah (Gen.3:15), and certain vital aspects of that precious ministry had been revealed to David her tutor's father. Thus, submissive to God's will though he was how appalling was the stress under which Isaac lay, his heart like wax, prayer his source of comfort (Ps.22:9-11,14); the knife within reach.

Then he saw it, held high and tightly in his father's hand, the dazzling rays of the sun dancing on the blade, as it menacingly hovered above his heart (Gen.22:10). This was no masquerade, an act, the intensity of his father's expression revealed that. Nor could restraint be hoped for, or expected; it was as if his father had forsaken him (Ps.22:1), driven on intent upon seeing his son finish the work he had been called to fulfil (John 17:3). There was no turning back. Abraham looked down at his son; his son looked up to heaven.

Then suddenly as the blade was about to make its final plunge, a voice was heard breaking into the anguished silence. Abraham heard his name, the knife losing interest in its victim, as the Patriarch reacted to the One he knew so well. It was the Angel of the Lord, his Friend from heaven, who had observed the dramatic scene, and now terminated the trauma (Gen.22:11).

How eager was Abraham to lay aside his knife, and the 'lad' to be set free, as the old man listened to the words of commendation: 'now I know that thou fearest God, seeing thou hast not withheld thy son, thine only son from me' (Gen.22:12). Exhausted and no doubt trembling with relief and joy, the two were in great need of rest. How close Isaac had been to death; how close Abraham had been to bringing it about!

But in Isaac's rescue from certain death there was only a partial fulfilment of the parable enacted on Mount Moriah; while breathing sighs of relief he learned (the hard way) the vital importance of a substitute to take the sinner's place, as no doubt Sheba did in her quest after truth when Solomon related the account to her as assuredly he must have done. Would she not have learned what the 'burnt offering' signified, the sacrifice being offered to God to appease his anger against sin 'and for uncleanness' (Zech.13:1), that 'it is the blood that maketh an atonement for the soul' (Lev.17:11)? Whose blood? Not the sinner's, but one taking his place under the weight of divine judgment: an animal's blood.

Suddenly, as Abraham and Isaac were recovering from the experience through which they had passed, the old Patriarch saw the necessary substitute. It was a ram. Its bleating probably attracted his attention, because it was caught up in a thicket by its horns (Gen.22:13): the substitute to take Isaac's place!

Five things could have occurred to Isaac as he thought about the incident, and also to Sheba when told about it. When he was staring anxiously at the blade of the knife about to plummet into his chest, and the voice of the Divine had called out, it was more-than-likely the first time he had heard it.

Then again, upon thinking about the commendation of Abraham by the angel of the Lord – 'now I know that thou fearest God, seeing thou hast not withheld thy son, thine only son from me' (Gen.22:12)

– how extraordinary had been those words. Had not his father 'feared' God prior to his arrival at Moriah? Yes of course he had, but the testing of such claims is necessary to prove their worth (Acts 14:22). Now both heaven and earth knew the greatness of his father's faith, and obedience to God (Gal.3:9). He ACTUALLY was about to die, and his father REALLY was about to kill him! Equally, upon reflection, how thankful he was to be rescued and how grateful to the ram! And as he watched his father kill the animal, lay its carcase upon the wood and offer it IN HIS STEAD to God, one phrase must surely have been uppermost in his mind: 'that could have been ME!' Then another thought: it was God who 'found' the ram when the need arose. Isaac did not even have to chase it, and his aged father would not have been capable of doing so. The Lord had made sure the thicket prevented an escape. But then, the sacrificial Lamb of God had no avenue for escape or hope of rescue either; these were also sacrificed, in favour of the Father's will and purpose (Matt.26:39,53).

No doubt Abraham and his son watched in silence as the flames ravished the remains of the beast, the odour of burning flesh hanging like a cloud over them. Slowly, very slowly, the carcase sizzled to a frazzle until there was more ash than substance. It is not known what thoughts were theirs, except that the Lord's provision of a substitute for Isaac would have featured prominently. Abraham named the venue that had witnessed such emotional and spiritual trauma, 'Jehovah-jireh', and his son would certainly have approved: 'the Lord will provide', and he had, wonderfully (Gen.22:14).

The silence was suddenly broken; the Voice again interrupted their train of thought. If father and son were thankful, they were also about to be greatly encouraged. Clearly, heaven was impressed with what had occurred on the mount that day, 'because thou hast done this thing, and hast not withheld thy son, thine only son' (Gen.22:16). How vitally important was that concept to heaven, and how relevant to Sheba's quest. The purposes of grace were, of course, already known in eternity, that a beloved only Son (Matt. 17:5) would not be 'withheld' and would die in the stead of sinners (John 3:16).

HOMEWARD BOUND

So, Abraham and Isaac turned their backs upon the land of Moriah, with a lighter step than they had upon their arrival, the catalogue of divine promises still ringing in their ears: personal, national and universal. More than thirty years had passed since the pre-existent Christ had first appeared at Abraham's side (although known at that time as Abram, Gen.12:1-3), and now with the astonishing demonstration of faith and obedience that heaven had witnessed, the apex of their relationship had been reached. As a result, the Lord would pour out his beneficence upon his faithful 'friend' (2 Chron.20:7; James 2:23); upon the myriads who would descend from him (as numerous as the stars in the sky, and the sand on the beach), and indeed, upon the entire earth (Gen.22:15-18).

In short, Sheba's 'hard' questioning was gradually being satisfied (1 Kings 10:1). A day would dawn when a beloved only Son from heaven would be offered as a sacrifice to God, a ministry reaping benefit for the entire earth. This Son would arrive as fully human, because he was to arise from a mighty nation that had descended from Abraham, Isaac being the first in the long line.

At last the father and son re-joined the two patient employees, whose curiosity must have been aroused still further by the long absence. They would also have noticed that Abraham and Isaac were more joyful than when they had departed on their journey. But, unlike Sheba, their curiosity was never satisfied. Back home to Beersheba they travelled, another three long and arduous days (Gen.22:4), but if throughout the journey the servants remained puzzled, the rejoicing of the old man and his son continued unabated. What a great deal they had to tell Sarah!

SECTION
TWO

'...the house of the Lord at Jerusalem in mount Moriah...'
(2 Chron. 3:1)

SEVEN
Ascent to the House of the Lord

Along the palace corridors whispers could surely be heard; gossip and rumours. Jehoshaphat the official recorder (1 Kings 4:3) implies that the meetings between Solomon and Sheba were lengthy and held in private: 'communing' is not for the public gaze, and one cannot be brief when withholding nothing from the heart (1 Kings 10:2). So what was going on behind those closed doors, on so many occasions, and for long periods? There would have been much speculation, and many secret smiles. But only one person appeared to know, and Jehoshaphat was in no doubt the fellowship the King and the visiting Queen were enjoying was not of a romantic kind but rather was of a spiritual nature.

As already noted, they would have spent much time discussing Abraham to whom they were both racially related. They travelled with him, from Ur of the Chaldees to Canaan (Gen.12:1-6) and on to Mount Moriah (Gen.22), and with Moses and the Israelites from Mount Sinai and the giving of the law (Exod.19-20) to Mount Nebo where they viewed the land of promise (Deut.34:1-4). They observed Joshua and the people enter that land (Josh.3), and the tribes claim their inheritance (Josh.13-21). Then the messianic prophesies, about which Solomon would have had a limited understanding: in Eden (Gen.3:15), in the desert (Deut.18:15), even from the enemy's mouth (Numb.24:15-17), and in his father David's court (2 Sam.7:16).

FROM CLOSED DOORS TO OPENED EYES

The lessons however were not only learned from within the confines of the palace walls, but beyond them. During her stay in Jerusalem Sheba had an opportunity, not only to listen to Solomon, but also to observe his personal devotion to the great God of Israel: 'his ascent by which he went up unto the house of the Lord' (1 Kings 10:5). Clearly, the king's renowned wisdom was not merely of the mind and mouth, but of the heart, his teaching not merely academic but experiential.

Had Sheba been present at the inauguration of worship within Jerusalem's recently built temple (2 Chron.3:2), when Solomon had movingly led the people to Jehovah's throne in prayer, she would have noted the depth of his devotion (1 Kings 8). How elevated was his view of God ('the heaven and heaven of heavens cannot contain thee', v.27): his majesty without equal ('there is no God like thee, in heaven above, or on earth beneath', v.23), his sovereignty awesome ('thy strong hand…thy stretched out arm', v.42), his exalted name ('thy great name', v.42), his righteousness unceasing ('thine eyes may be open toward this house night and day', v.29), his covenantal faithfulness and immeasurable mercy ('who keepest covenant and mercy with thy servants that walk before thee with all their heart', v.23).

And Solomon would not have shed these mighty truths when leaving the temple precincts, but was adorned with them at all times, certainly during the period of Sheba's visitation. When in her presence, and when solemnly in procession ascending to the house of the Lord, the aura of heaven's omnipotence remained. She could not help but be very impressed (1 Kings 10:5).

Sheba must also have been aware that Solomon's regular appearance at the temple was not a mere formality, a king seeking popular approval, but was in fact an act of genuine devotion. He feared God, and at that stage at least (1 Kings 11:1-13), was obedient to him because, as he placed on record, to do so 'is the whole duty of man' for which he must give account to God (Eccles.12:13,14).

As the people sought their king's wisdom (1 Kings 10:8), so equally they were influenced by his example (Prov.8:33,34). They knew that when a youth he had 'remembered' his Creator (Eccles. 12:1), and that their nation's extraordinary spiritual and economic prosperity (2 Chron.1:12) were due to their sovereign's unique relationship with Jehovah even as 'a little child' (1 Kings 3:7). Sheba was learning this too.

She was also learning that attendance at Jehovah's house was completely unlike anything she and her people had ever experienced. Back home at Marib, did they believe their god Ilumquh understood 'every secret thing' about them, or cared (Eccles.12:14)? Had they, therefore, a need to prepare their hearts prior to appearing before their god? But Jehovah, the great and everlasting God of Israel (Jer.10:10), demanded it!

Thus, behind the devotional intensity of the King's ascent to the house of the Lord lay a solemn duty within the privacy of his own. Not for him and his people the careless approach to the worship of a holy God, a failure to 'hear', a 'sacrifice of fools'. Rather, he and his people 'watched their step'; their mouths and hearts in prayer (Eccles.5:1). How different was all this from what took place at Marib!

ON MOUNT MORIAH

In the light of that could she have resisted from requesting to be shown the temple, so closely associated with the King it is to this day still referred to as 'Solomon's temple', and would he have refused? Indeed, so proud was he of it, that even in the presence of Jehovah, he attributed its erection to himself (1 Kings 8:27)! Probably, the suggestion of a sightseeing walk to this magnificent place of worship came from him in the first place.

They would not have had far to go, a few hundred yards (the sites where the temple and his palace once stood can still be seen), but far enough for Sheba to have collected her thoughts. She was by this time already well acquainted with the luxuriant delights discovered in the palace (1 Kings 10:4-8), and may have mused upon the fact that it had taken thirteen years to build. That is, almost twice as long as the house of his God, and much smaller too (1 Kings 6:38; 7:1,2)!

But apart from probably having seen the temple from her apartment in the palace (it was near enough for her to have done so), her curiosity aroused, there was something else that fascinated Sheba about the location: its historic associations with Solomon and his people. It was situated upon Mount Moriah, about which she had been hearing so much (2 Chron.3:1). She was now in the land of Moriah!

So this was where Abraham came at God's command, where Isaac lay upon the altar under the threat of the knife, and where the ram was sacrificed as a substitute. Sheba would have been as interested as many a tourist today, but when the significance of the narrative has been explained, how much more appealing is the account. There can be little doubt that in their 'communing' with each other (1 Kings 10:2), it being such a vital aspect of her quest, Solomon would have delighted to help her understand the story.

UNHEARD NOISE

Before her arrival at the site (where a mosque, 'the Dome of the Rock', now stands), Sheba would undoubtedly have enquired about the history of such a wonderful building as Jerusalem's famous temple, whose apex reached high above her. Solomon would proudly have informed her that the desire to erect such a building, the house for the Lord, had been his father's.

On one occasion, David had been enjoying the comforts of his beautiful palace - 'a house of cedars' - when the thought came to him which he expressed to his prophet Nathan, that by contrast, so sacred a symbol of God's presence as the ark of the covenant was situated in the tent which David had ordered to be pitched for it (1 Chron.16:1). A more suitable house was required for Jehovah.

But just hours later Nathan had revealed to him, that the construction of the temple was not to be in the hands of the King, but rather of Solomon his son (1 Chron.17:1-4). Some time afterwards David learned why: 'Thou hast shed blood abundantly, and hast made great wars' (1 Chron.22:8). Carnality and spirituality were not to collide (Rom.8:8), but David must have felt the blow.

Nevertheless, such was his passion for the project – 'my affection to the house of my God' (1 Chron.29:3) - even if he was not permitted to be responsible for the building's construction, behind the scenes he organised its preparation. In a flurry of activity, he collated an enormous amount of precious metals, and immense quantities of brass (18,000 talents) and iron (100,000) from the ruling classes, affected by their sovereign's enthusiasm. Others also joined in the euphoria, adding to the general largesse, and contributing sacrificially to the treasury (1 Chron.29:6-9). The experience was reminiscent of the spirit behind the establishing of tabernacle worship during the Israelites' wilderness wanderings (Exod.35:5). The generosity even arrived from across the border, a large amount of timber being sent from Tyre (1 Kings 5:1,10-12) and Sidon (1 Chron.22:4), as a result of David's friendship and Solomon's agreement with King Hiram of Tyre.

His father's zeal for the HOUSE of the Lord was undoubted - exemplified a thousand years later by 'the Son of David' (John 2:17), which David himself had foretold (Ps.69:9) – but if possible Solomon's vision of the temple's GLORY must have reached even greater heights. Years before during the country's blackest period, that of the judges, the name 'Ichabod' ('the glory is departed from Israel') was written across her people (1 Sam.4:21); but when the temple was completed another name would be found there, the most glorious name of all, that of Israel's mighty God (1 Kings 8:29).

For that reason no expense was spared: 100,000 talents of gold and 'a thousand thousand talents of silver' (1 Chron.22:14). David, under divine inspiration, even marked out the spot where the building would stand; how could he, of all people, overlook Ornan's threshing floor (1 Chron.21:18-27; 2 Chron.3:1)? He even drew up the plans for the temple's construction.

Then, the entire city of Jerusalem blossomed into a hive of activity, as the building programme got under way (1 Kings 5:13-18). It was 969BC, and the fourth year of Solomon's exciting reign

(1 Kings 6:1; 2 Chron.3:2). In a remarkable display of organisational skill 183,000 men (1 Kings 5:13-15), were summoned to the toil, whose labour was by no means a freewill offering unto the Lord (there were 3,300 overseers!), in fact they considered their conscription to the task a very 'heavy yoke' indeed (1 Kings 12:10). They had no choice: 30,000 Israelites (10,000 per month in rotation), and 153,000 conquered Canaanites, of whom 70,000 were allotted to carry heavy materials as well as 80,000 who were carpenters or masons. So, the building programme was set in motion as many thousands of men dug, hammered, carried, cut or carved. They sweated and heaved, pulled and pushed, grunted and groaned; orders were shouted, and instructions given.

However, Jehoshaphat the Recorder presented the world with a tantalising mystery: 'the house (of the Lord), when it was in building, was built of stone made ready before it was brought thither, so that there was neither hammer nor axe nor any tool of iron heard in the house, while it was in building' (1 Kings 6:7). Thousands of men toiling with hammers, axes and iron tools, and yet not heard doing so!

But why was the stone prepared away from the site, where was it prepared, and why was all that noise not heard? For centuries the questions kept scholars speculating. Sheba would have known the answers, having learned them from Solomon, but it was only in the 20th century that the rest of the world knew too. One day a dog disappeared from view into undergrowth not far from the temple mount, Mount Moriah, and the dog's owner scrambled in after it. In searching, to his amazement he found himself inside a huge cave where, despite the passing of the centuries, could be seen stonework and the evidence of a great deal of activity. It was as if the day's toil had just ended in the 'royal caverns'.

The noise then could not be heard because the work was carried out underground, in what became known as 'Solomon's Quarries', which was why the huge stones were dragged to the site of the temple. The stonework was carried out where it had been quarried because limestone is naturally soft and therefore easily worked upon, whereas it hardens very quickly in the heat.

A HOUSE, UNTO THE NAME OF THE LORD

Apart from learning that initially it had been David's idea to build the temple, there were several other interesting facets about it that would have fascinated Sheba. Undoubtedly, the first was the position of the building. In all other lands including her own, the sun was central to national and religious adoration. Sheba must, therefore, have suffered something of a cultural shock to discover that Jerusalem's temple, like the tabernacle in the wilderness before it, although it faced east from where the sun rose each morning (Num.3:23), it meant that as the Monarch, the priests, the Levites and the people ascended to the temple mount to do business with almighty God, their backs were towards the sun. Thus they were constantly reminded that the nation had also turned its back upon heathen worship. How many more 'hard questions' must Sheba have asked upon hearing this!

Yet, despite Israel's antipathy towards idolatrous religions like her own, Sheba may have been quietly surprised to discover that the materials for the building of the temple as well as the architects and craftsmen for the work had not primarily been found locally, but were imported from neighbouring Phoenicia. However, this had been a wise move. King Hiram, through whose influence Tyre was celebrated for its wealth and magnificence, had befriended Solomon's father. It was just as well. Israel's reputation as a fighting machine, and David's prowess as its leader, made it a necessity to be on good terms with Israel. The situation had not changed when the temple was built.

Thus Hiram agreed to send what was required, in exchange for generous provision: of wheat and barley 20,000 measures apiece, and likewise of wine and oil 20,000 'baths' each (2 Chron. 2:10) a 'bath' equalling 5.8 gallons. Soon, a large amount of stone quarried in Lebanon was transported back to Israel by many of the 70,000 Canaanites used as manual labourers. But also, and particularly, 'timber in abundance': fir trees, algum (cypress) trees and the famed cedars (2 Chron. 2:8). No finer could one find as building material than the cedars of Lebanon, 'the trees of the Lord...full of sap'

(Ps.104:16); no better carpenters and masons either than those who arrived from Tyre to assist the craftsmen of Israel. David's palace had been built under a similar agreement (2 Sam.5:11). At Solomon's request, Hiram even provided a leading expert on gold, silver, brass, 'purple and crimson, and blue' (2 Chron.2:7,14).

As far as Sheba was concerned the seven years of expertise coupled to great toil had all been worthwhile (1 Kings 6:38; 10:5). How magnificent the house of Jehovah must have appeared to her, bathed as it was throughout the day by the sun's dazzling white light, the irony of which would not have gone unnoticed by her. Jerusalem was 2,500 feet above sea level, and the temple stood majestically on the mount much higher than that, and could be seen from afar and was the envy of Israel's neighbours.

Its stonework gleamed in the brightness of the day, and as Sheba stood to admire it, its height rising above her towards the heavens, she could not but have compared it with the temples back home; compared the religion of the kingdom of Israel with that of the kingdom of Sheba; compared the glory of Jehovah with that of the moon god (Is.42:8). The Queen would have been even more impressed had she known, or anyone involved in the temple's construction for that matter, that it was destined to stand there for over four centuries (although it was plundered only thirty years later, 1 Kings 14:25,26).

Comparisons with the temple of Ezekiel's vision (40-46) suggests Solomon's stood on a platform, but in any case following the scriptural pattern, it was situated within a large courtyard ('the great court') consisting of three rows of carved stones 'and a row of cedar beams' (1 Kings 7:12), and before the temple was another very special area where the priests offered up the animal sacrifices assisted by the Levites (Lev.1:3).

Upon the sides and rear of the temple was an additional building consisting of three levels, each nearly eight feet high, and used for storage. From the bottom to the top the width of each level increased: the first was seven and a half feet wide, the second nine feet, and the third ten and a half. A flight of steps led to each level. This structure was about half the height of the temple, and though built against the walls, was not fastened to them. It was divided into apartments, which opened into the gallery that surrounded it. (1 Kings 6:1-8).

The dimensions of the temple itself were ninety feet by thirty (2 Chron.3:3), as already mentioned, considerably smaller than Solomon's palace! However, the tabernacle and the temple shared the same basic design, which was not surprising as it had originally been revealed from heaven (Exod.25:9). That is, they were divided into two sections, the Holy Place (occupied by the altar of incense, the table of shewbread and the seven-branched candlestick) and the Most Holy Place (where stood the sacred ark of the covenant in solitary isolation), separated in the tabernacle by a veil (Exod.26: 33) and in the temple by sturdy doors made from the wood of olive trees (1 Kings 6:31).

There were other differences too, between the layout of the tabernacle and that of the temple, which reflected the Israelites' transition from the primitive to the sophisticated; from being wilderness wanderers to that of citizens of an established kingdom; from walking upon sand to working with luxury. Everything to do with the temple was on a grand scale, materially dwarfing the tabernacle into an apparent insignificance, underlining the greater spiritual depth that lay behind the simplicity of the tabernacle.

To begin with the temple was exactly twice its size, with the altar of burnt offering in 'the court of the priests' being a massive thirty feet square and fifteen feet high. For the priests to be able to use it steps would have been required, in which case, in seeking religious grandeur God's command had been violated (Exod.21: 26). Also in that court, the tabernacle's laver filled with water for the priests' use that stood between the Holy Place and the altar, in the temple was multiplied tenfold. From being a fairly ordinary vessel of polished brass, the ten rested on bases depicting various animals.

The lavers were so vast (each fifteen feet in diameter, seven and a half feet high) it was not surprising they were called 'seas' (1 Kings 7:38,39; 2 Chron.4:6).

Again, whereas a four-coloured embroidered cloth covered the entrance to the tabernacle's Holy place, a porch measuring thirty feet wide by fifteen feet deep marked the entrance of the Holy Place of the temple, complete with two named bronze pillars (1 Kings 7:15-21). Within, instead of one seven-branched candlestick and table of shewbread (Exod.25:23-37), there were ten of each (1 Kings 7:48; 2 Chron.4:8)! And likewise, the Most Holy Place: whereas in the tabernacle there were two fairly small cherubim overshadowing the sacred ark (Exod.25:18-20), the temple olivewood cherubim overlaid with gold leaf were fifteen feet tall (1 Kings 6:23-28; 2 Chron. 3:10-13)!

Add to all this the luxuriant and brightly colourful display of fine gold, silver, burnished bronze, the splendid woodwork and the fact that the building was 'garnished....with precious stones for beauty' (2 Chron.3:6), when she heard about it (for she would not have been permitted to enter the building) how could Sheba have been other than astonished, and desirous of wanting to learn more? Not merely out of curiosity, but because in her quest for understanding about 'the name of the Lord' she must have realised the secret lay somewhere inside this temple dedicated to Jehovah (at the opening of which 22,000 oxen and 120,000 sheep were sacrificed in his praise and thanksgiving. 1 Kings 8:63), and particularly within the tabernacle that preceded it.

What mystery lay behind those words (from a God who actually speaks! Jer.10: 5), that he intended to live among the Israelites (Exod.25:9)? Surely, in that astonishing revelation could be discovered what she sought.

EIGHT
Marvellous Works and Wonders

But first, Solomon had a story to tell, and a visitor to Israel was a captured audience. Sheba would not have been an exception. In her quest she had already heard important aspects of it, but in understanding the secrets the temple had to reveal Solomon would have felt obliged to tell the remarkable story of his people's meeting with God at Mount Sinai (Exod.19). Yes, with the true God, the great God of Israel.

She would have learned how Joseph, one of Abraham's great grandsons, found himself in Egypt and of his remarkable rise to prominence in that country, 'the land of Ham' (Mizraim), where after the flood Noah's son settled (Gen.10:6; Ps.105:23). Eventually Joseph's father Jacob, the son of Isaac, took his family to Egypt during a terrible period of famine (Gen.37-46).

DRAWN TO THE BUSH

It was in that land Moses was born at a time when Pharaoh was persecuting the Hebrews, demanding the death of newborn boys, lest in adulthood they should prove a formidable 'fifth column' (Exod.1:7-16). His mother Jochebed hid her three month old son in a basket made from bulrushes (Exod.6:20; Acts 7:20), but he was found by Pharaoh's daughter, and although in a wonderful providence Jochebed raised him on her behalf (and was paid for doing so!), the day arrived when she felt obliged to hand her son over to his royal adopted mother (Exod.1-2).

Forty years passed, during which time Moses was educated as an Egyptian aristocrat (Acts 7:22), until one particular incident revealed his true birth. In seeing an Egyptian hit a Hebrew his instinct drove him to choose sides; he killed the Egyptian and was seen doing so. Moses left the country hurriedly under a threat from Pharaoh (Exod.2:11-15).

Another forty years went by (Exod.7:7; Acts 7:30), years spent as a shepherd in the land of Midian, when one day he experienced an extraordinary phenomenon. While in the desert with a flock of sheep belonging to his father-in-law he saw a strange sight, a burning bush that remained untouched by the flames. Upon closer inspection he received a shock, similar to that which Abraham initially must have had (Gen.12:1), because the same Lord manifested himself; 'the God of glory' (Exod.3:4; Acts 7:2).

Abraham was made aware of the phrase 'I will' (Gen.12: 2,3), Moses of 'I AM' (Exod.3:14) which upon enquiring he discovered was the name of this Figure in the flames (Dan.3:25; John 8:58). He quickly learned the reason behind the visitation. Abraham had been commanded to journey to an unknown Promised Land (Gen.12:1), but he to return to a very well-known and unpromising land, Egypt; Abraham to produce a 'great nation' (Gen.12:2), Moses to rescue it (Exod.3:7-10).

And this he did, after Pharaoh had heard God's message 'Let my people go', and a series of judgments had been poured out upon the country (Exod.5:1; 7-12). The final one was the bitterest of all, the death of the firstborn, even in the palace; every home in the land, and even among the cattle (Exod.11:5). Egypt was brought to its knees (Exod.10:7). God's people though were sheltered from the divine onslaught, the blood of a slaughtered young male lamb having been sprinkled on 'the two side posts and on the upper door post' of each home (Exod.12:7). No creature - whether human or animal - can give more than his blood, his life, the ultimate sacrifice (Lev.17:11). Thus Sheba learned, as the Hebrews did that remarkable night, the value and uniqueness of atonement. She would have been reminded again of Isaac, the young 'lad', and the altar his father had built.

So the nation (consisting of about 2,000,000 people) triumphantly left the country of its adoption with its herds and flocks after 430 years (Exod.12:40,42). Travelling with them, carried reverently in a casket, were the bones of Abraham's great grandson Joseph (Exod.13:19), who had requested that in his death he should journey with his people (Gen.50:25). Headed by Moses, and no doubt his brother Aaron (Exod.5:1), this strange procession like a giant snake very slowly moved out of the area, prayerful yearning having given way to sombre expectation (Exod.2:23): the dignified officers, the thoughtful elderly, the anxious parents, the excited children, the slow-moving cattle, the nervous flocks, and the creaking wagons.

But before them hovered a mysterious cloud, bright with a glorious radiance (Exod.13:21), a sight that surely baffled the Egyptians still further.

A people that had witnessed such trauma albeit upon their enemies among whom they lived, ten alarming 'wonders in the land of Egypt' (Exod.7:3), could not be expected to be other than triumphant yet grave. The entire country broken upon the 'wheel' of God's displeasure: water turned into blood; the land infested in their turn with frogs, lice, flies and locusts; both man and beast diseased; the elements mirroring fearful anger in thunders, lightning and darkness; the anguished cries of mourning in every home (Exod.7-12).

How special were these refugees (Deut.7:6-8), that under the protection of blood-sacrifice (Exod.12:13), they had escaped heaven's vengeance (2 Thess.1:8-10). They had therefore no need to fear the future, despite how uncertain it seemed as they turned their backs upon the past and crossed the sand to the unknown. The mighty I AM had miraculously rescued them through Moses' anointed leadership, and whether they knew it or not, they must have realised there was a purpose in view behind the extraordinary events through which they were passing (Exod. 3:14,17).

It soon became clear in which direction this vast multitude was to head (Exod.14:2), not through the warlike territory of Philistia because slavery had not equipped them for warfare. Instead, the mysterious cloud glided the procession to what must have seemed an even starker situation, 'the wilderness of the Red Sea' (Exod.13:17-22). They arrived that first evening at the end of stage one of their epic journey to discover that if their backs were turned towards slavery, their faces were confronted by sea!

They possessed no boats, crafts or rafts of any kind. They were familiar with sand, not sea, and besides, with many thousands of people and livestock in their company not even Noah and his ark could have catered for their needs at that moment. They could not go forward; they dared not go back. They were trapped.

Unease must have spread rapidly through the ranks of this great multitude, the triumphant confidence felt shortly before evaporating. Questioning doubt would have flown in every direction: was God really guiding them, and if so, why had he led them to a cul-de-sac? Perhaps Moses had misinterpreted the message. Already, God's people had learned three valuable lessons in their journey with him: circumstances are not always what they appear to be, what on the surface is bewildering need not necessarily be so, and that behind even the darkest of uncertainties lies the practical purposes of God.

DRAWN TO THE SEA

But Moses knew why they had encamped in such an awkward place, and no doubt Aaron and probably his sister Miriam too for she was a prophetess living close to God (Exod.15:20). He never leads his people astray (Rom.8:28). The reason why he appeared to have done so on this occasion, was to pave the way for one of the great miracles known to mankind. God intended to be 'honoured upon Pharaoh, and upon all his host' (Exod.14:3,4); to brand his sovereign name, the 'name of the Lord' (1 Kings 10:1), upon the despot and his subjects, and in doing so, have his awesome power placed on record in the annals of history (Rom.9: 17). God will never permit his glory to be given to another (Is.42:8), and reacts accordingly when the attempt is made (Ezek. 6:4).

In the meantime as God's people gazed across the sea, the twilight in a strange environment creating its own unease, they wondered what would happen next. Pharaoh on the other hand gazed across the sand wondering what he had done. The slaves were free! It was as if he had just awoken from a nightmare. 'Why have we done this...? (Exod.14:5)'; not a few of them, but a nation so large it had seemingly filled the entire country (Exod.1:7-11). Now they were gone and Egyptian pride was smarting, the old fears returned, particularly within the palace.

The fear of Pharaoh's predecessor had been that the multitudes of the Hebrews in the land would prove a political danger, joining forces in the event of a war with Egypt's enemies. Thus the policy adopted was to enslave these 'strangers' in their midst (Exod.1:10,11). That policy had not changed, and nor had the fears, in fact the latter had increased. Now that they were heading towards the country's border these slaves, angry at their treatment throughout many years, might well find common cause with troublesome neighbours.

There was only one thing to do; the slaves would have to be brought back, an action that should not prove too difficult to carry out. They were not armed. What could they do against the might of the Egyptian military? Pharaoh was very confident but what he did not, and could not have known, was that there was another power within his palace much greater than his (Rom.9:17). I AM, the mighty God of the Hebrews (Exod.3:14), who not long before had left his giant 'footprints' in Egypt's soil (Exod.7-12), had performed two more miracles without Pharaoh knowing about it. When he was guiding the Hebrews OUT of Egypt, he was also guiding events from WITHIN the country too! Omnipresence was not a truth either side knew about, that God cannot be avoided wherever one wanders (Jer.23:24). He was without and within Egypt, and at the same time. David had taught this to Solomon; Solomon to Sheba (Ps.139:7-12).

The second miracle concerned Pharaoh himself, the most powerful man in the known world. He had already snuffed out the candle and shut the door against the Hebrews' God – 'Who is the

Lord, that I should obey his voice.....? (Exod.5:2)' – but Jehovah locked that 'door', making his antagonist's heart even harder (Exod.14:4). The situation could not be altered. God drove Pharaoh to the abyss: many centuries later Judas was driven there too (John 13:2). But it is the way of the wicked to believe they captain their own lives, do as they wish, a belief that places them in a foolish position (Luke 12:16-21). The army officers gave their orders, the troops were mustered, the horses made ready, and as many as 600 chariots assembled (Exod.14:9): all at the command of one controlled by the God he vowed never to obey (Exod.5:2; Rom.9: 17)!

It was an impressive sight. Hundreds of horses regaled in their bridles and feathered headgear, pulling every chariot Egypt possessed (Exod.14:9), and mastered by highly trained warriors, poured out through the gates of the city and drummed their way at a gallop across the desert. Pharaoh himself led the charge, a most unusual thing to do outside of a war situation. But this was a unique occasion. He was determined to wreak vengeance upon those who had made a fool of him before his subjects. He who demanded abject obeisance from everyone had been outwitted, not even by his own people, but by unwanted foreigners, and slaves at that (Exod.10:7). He had been humiliated, and pride drove him to meet with destiny (Exod.15:19). And yet, was there not in this display a measure of 'over-kill'? True, there were about 2,000,000 freed slaves to be rounded up and returned to Egypt, but they were defenceless and mainly consisted of women and children (Exod.12: 37). Would it have needed at least 600 troops to complete the task, or twice that number if each chariot contained two men? In any case, the fact that 'all the chariots of Egypt' were employed appears to reveal there was more to this campaign than just the recapturing of slaves. The chariots - the entire stock (Exod.14:7) - were normally stored away in the event of a war, and on this occasion every one of them was brought out as if the country had been called to arms. It was clear Pharaoh and his officials considered the situation with the Hebrews as threatening as any enemy from across the border.

The reason for the show of strength was fear. Fear because of what had recently happened, the country ravaged by disasters (Exod.10:7) incurred by the strange miraculous powers of the Hebrew leader (Exod.7-12). But also, fears for what might result from hindering his departure from the area, and in seeking to force the multitudes with him to return. What further alarming manifestations would Pharaoh and his men witness? It reveals how determined was he to retrieve his slaves, and to recover his shattered pride, that to get his way he was prepared to confront Mystery head-on. It also emphasises the fact that the citizens of God's 'holy nation' have always been very special to him, and thus are a remarkable people (Deut.7:6-8; 1 Peter 2:9).

Jehovah's children looked forlornly out to sea, or as families huddled together despondently in their tents. Then suddenly the rumbling of 1,200 spinning wheels were heard, and chariots sighted on the horizon, clouds of sand and dust following in their wake. They must have seemed as locusts swarming towards them, more menacing as the moments flew by. Terror rippled through the encampment as a chilling breeze, the sea by contrast appearing both calm and comforting. The Hebrews knew instinctively where to turn, circumstances having driven them there incessantly throughout their unhappy lives (Exod.2:23): to God (Exod.14:10). Where else would his children want to be at such a fearful time as this (Is.26:4)?

But the multitude beside the sea was 'mixed' (Exod.12:38). There were some among the Hebrews who had even more reasons to fear, and yet were unable to call upon Jehovah to help them, because they had no filial claim upon him. They were Egyptians who had fled from their country's disaster zone, and had mingled with the Pharaoh's enemies in the hope of finding protection.

Provision was later made for them (Exod.22:21), God's people sternly warned not to persecute these strangers (Exod.23: 9), in fact to treat the stranger 'as one born among you' (Lev.19: 34), indeed to love him (Deut.10:19). It was as well these commands were given, because the newcomers later caused problems when the hardships of the desert wanderings had to be endured (Numb.11:4).

Then, as often happens when God's people are distraught, having humbly sought his ear and aid they then belligerently cast their fears into his servant's face, revealing how thin is the line between adulation and disillusionment. How pitiful had been the yearning to escape from the land of their bondage (Exod.2:23), and how grateful they were for Moses' appearance in answer to their prayers, but now when in distress all that had conveniently been overlooked. After all Moses and his brother courageously endured when confronting Pharaoh, the people brushed aside in suggesting it would have been better had they remained as slaves (Exod.3:11). Then having displayed a lack of faith in the purposes of God and trust in his choice of a deliverer, in seeking to justify themselves they suggested that Moses should have listened to them in first place (Exod.14:10-12)!

But what they had also overlooked was how tenuous had been their hold upon faith from the start. With what joy they had received Aaron's news on behalf of his brother (for Moses suffered from a speech impediment, Exod.4:10) that God was about to rescue his people; how fervently at first they believed it (Exod.4: 29-31), and how swift they were to doubt (Exod.5:20,21)! And despite the evidences of God's power and grace, the land of their bondage having been devastated on their behalf (Exod.7-12), lurking just beneath their triumphant entrance into the longed-for freedom was that same doubt. But Moses received the blame.

However, he bore the hurt courageously, with the meekness for which he is known (Numb.12:3). The incident though revealed the greatness of Jehovah's servant. He stood alone (except, perhaps, for his sister Miriam) with the Egyptian military rapidly approaching, and even an entire nation of his own fearful and angry people against him. At that stage, even his brother Aaron was proving fickle (Exod.32:2-6). Yet, with apparent calmness Moses strode confidently to the water's edge, in sharp contrast to the trembling of his people, the sounds of the rumbling wheels ominously reaching a thunderous crescendo in the background. Time was not to spare, soon the encampment would reverberate with the sounds of angry voices and shrill screams.

But seemingly oblivious to the terror that filled the air Moses turned towards the people; a people soured by his leadership earlier (Exod.14:11,12), but now solely dependent upon it as never before. His appearance in the circumstances was heroic, his message as brief as time permitted, and both would have seemed surreal to his vast audience. With the shadow of violence looming large behind them, and the depth of a watery grave before them, Moses commanded them not to fear. Those who desperately wanted to run, although there was nowhere to go, were told to stand still!

Then suddenly, they whose faith was buried in the sand and whose fear was fever-pitched, anxious at the approaching doom and the forthcoming gloom were suddenly transported heavenward. With just a handful of words, and the exercise of a giant faith, Moses revealed heaven's agenda: 'the Lord shall fight for you' (Exod.14:14). How strange: they who had only recently witnessed God's triumph over Pharaoh on their behalf should not have expected him to do it again. They learned on that historic occasion, that for God's people to under-value his love for them is also to under-value his veracity.

And as if to shame them, and because of the value he placed upon the covenant (Deut.7:8) he had made with Abraham (Gen.12:1-3), ratified with Isaac (Gen.26:24) and with Jacob (Gen. 28:13 -15), the pursuing Egyptians would not be put to flight, they would be put to death (Exod.14:13,14). So many were in his audience not all could have heard his voice, but the message circulated swiftly from one individual to the next, and from tent to tent, until all assembled had realised that hope was near at hand. Of what kind they did not know, but if Jehovah was on their side who could possibly be against them, and succeed (Rom.8:31)?

Yet Moses himself was not without his private tremors. A leader, particularly of his magnitude, was not likely to weep on shoulders or quiver before those being led, nevertheless secretly and understandably having proclaimed his message there was a moment's hesitation. Yes, God was about to intervene and the pursuing Egyptians would be swept to perdition, but what happens next?

Of course, Moses knew, for he had just declared heroically 'see the salvation of the Lord, which he will shew to you today' (Exod.14:13), but the enormity of the miracle he and his people were about to witness caused the great man to hesitate. He would not have wanted the multitude to note his hesitancy, so turning from them he gazed out to sea, and from the depth of his heart cried to his unseen Lord standing beside him. His was a unique situation. Noah had also been called upon to demonstrate the sovereign power of God as well as the strength of his faith, and to an unbelieving and cynical people, but when the waters gushed from above and below the outstretching of Noah's hand had not been required (Gen.6).

Moses knew that is what he had to do at that precise moment, but it would appear for a 'split second' his faith flickered, and he heard a familiar voice: 'Wherefore criest thou unto me? Speak unto the children of Israel, that they GO FORWARD' (Exod.14:15). They could not have moved forward until the waters were parted, and this miracle would not have occurred before Moses had stretched forth the rod in his hand. So in commanding his servant to tell the people to proceed towards the sea, God was in fact saying to Moses 'Why are you hesitating? Stop crying to me, stretch out the rod! (Exod.14:15,16)'

But as he was about to do so, the nation watching in great anticipation, another miracle took place behind them. The mysterious Angel of the Lord who had appeared to Moses from among the flames of the burning bush forty years earlier (Exod.3: 2), and whose unseen presence had been the great source of comfort to him since, now swiftly moved behind the vast company. For the waiting Hebrews the only sign of this happening was, to their astonishment, the bright cloud towards which they had looked since being liberated silently changing direction and moving to their rear (Exod.13:21; 14:19; 40:36).

By this time, the chariots furiously driven were within a short distance of the prey, nightfall was fast approaching, and the command was given to set up camp. Time enough to deal with the Hebrews when dawn broke. Pharaoh and his men settled down for the night, although as they closed their eyes, they must have been puzzled by the strange 'pillar' of cloud that was moving towards them. So strange in fact, that had Pharaoh's pride not obscured his wisdom he might have recognised an omen when he saw one and ordered his men to retreat. One more miracle was one too many.

But they waited and slept, slept and waited, the stillness of the night disturbed only by the occasional neighing among the hundreds of horses who remained harnessed to the chariots. Then suddenly through the night air a cold breeze swept across the sands. The sleepers shivered, and sleep was disturbed. When eyes fully opened to an expected bright sunrise, they peered into the blackness of nightfall (Exod.14:20).

But earlier, close by, the prey had not experienced a similar discomfort. The night sky had sparkled with stars and the moon's reflection shimmered on the waters, yet to the Hebrews the expected nightfall had given way to daylight as the bright cloud of glory ('shechinah') over-shadowed them (Ps.105:39).

Fear surrendered to hope, anxiety to expectation, as the realisation broke over them all that Jehovah was at hand and had surely come to their rescue. They looked towards Moses, their belongings collected together ready for a swift departure from the scene, as hastily as their departure from Egypt had been (Exod.12: 11).

It was one of the most dramatic moments in history, and probably seemed as such to those present on that occasion, when Moses raised his arm towards the sea. In his hand was the rod of God, the insignia of his high calling (Rev.19:15), which had already demonstrated its powers to tragic effect back in Egypt (Ps.105:26-38). Now once more nature heeded the command of its Creator (Gen.1:3,4).

With God the Son, the Angel of the Lord, beside them what the Hebrews witnessed must have seemed to them as if they were present at the creation of all things, when as Solomon wrote, 'he strengthened the fountains of the deep; when he gave to the sea his decree, that the waters should not pass his commandment, when he appointed the foundations of the earth' (Prov.8:28,29).

Suddenly, the whistling of winds reaching to the shrillest of crescendos could be heard as it gusted across the Hebrew encampment towards the sea that stretched out before it; sand and desert dust that lay in its pathway swirled in all directions. All other sounds lost their relevance, including the voice of Moses, swallowed up as they were in the vortex of extraordinary power. The ruffled waters of the sea were 'stilled' (Ps.65:7), submissive to the divine energy that had hurtled towards them (Ps.89:9). It cut a swathe from shore to shore plunging to the sandy depths, until the sea split in two (Exod.14: 22), the waters rising to great heights on either side of what was now a wide track blown dry (Ps.74:15).

How fearful would the sight have been had not the glorious cloud bathed it in the brightness of Jehovah's presence (Neh.9:12), radiance resulting from it (Ps.104:2; John 12:46). Thus, the winds having abated, Moses clutching the rod of God like a shepherd's crook, stepped forward and walked between the mountainous watery walls (Exod.14:22) the people following like sheep (Ps.23: 4; Heb.11:29), no doubt timid at first as the initial step was taken, but with deepening confidence came rejoicing in their great God as they saw the fiery cloud drifting ahead of them leading the way (Pss.66:6; 144:15): the responsible officers, the tired elderly, the anxious youths, the relieved parents and their sleepy children (Ps. 146:5).

The procession was long and cumbersome, the frightened animals difficult to control, and therefore slow in crossing. How strong faith in God had to be. Those at the rear must surely have at times cast a furtive glance behind them, knowing that Pharaoh and hundreds of his warriors were within a very short chariot ride away, and what could have made them more uneasy was that with the absence of the cloud the view of the Egyptians would not be obscured when they awoke to what had happened (Ps.106:9).

And what of that restless water amassed on either side of them like tidal waves (Ps.78:13), whose ominous presence was constantly brought to the weary pilgrims' attention when sprinkled by it (1 Cor.10:1,2)? They were aware that only the divine beneficence towards them, Jehovah's 'glorious arm' (Is.63:12) for he delights to be with his people even 'in the uttermost parts of the sea' (Ps.139:9), restrained the raging sea from cascading devastatingly over them all.

They've gone! It could scarcely be believed, but the cry reverberated among the pursuing Egyptians, as bewildered charioteers and a tired and furious Pharaoh hastily clambered aboard their chariots. When they arrived at the bank and saw the neatly divided sea, yet another miracle, their immediate reaction is not recorded. Probably the soldiers shared their fellow citizens' desire to rid themselves of these strange and troublesome people (Exod.12:33; Ps.105:38), in which case it is possible they were reluctant to proceed further; that they were anxious to retreat.

But they had no choice in the matter, their king's pride saw to that. The might of Egypt's war machine therefore – 'all the chariots' (Exod.14:7) – thundered along the track opened up as a favour to others. Pharaoh was in possession of a hatred that blinded him to every other consideration, but what of the hundreds of his troops? What an extraordinary, and alarming, experience they were enduring. Apart from the strangeness of it all ('What are we doing, driving chariots in the middle of a sea?') there were those walls of water on either side of them, ominously straining to return to each other ('Any second now the whole lot could fall upon us').

And what of the 600, or more, horses; sensitive creatures to danger who surely balked at being driven furiously from the land into the sea, albeit on a dry pathway. How strenuously the men had to struggle with the reins; how often the whip was cracked, the eyes of the horses staring wildly with fright, their brave handlers shouting fiercely. Then the inevitable happened, which the charioteers would have foreseen and hence their reluctance to enter such a danger zone; the track was not as dry as it at first appeared to be. The ruffled waters had sprinkled the Hebrews as they had passed close by (1 Cor.10:1,2), but by now the pathway was saturated, the drenched sand churned up by hundreds of hooves and chariot wheels (Exod.14:25).

How dreadful was the moment when the practical and solemn truth dawned, 1,200 wheels were dragging to a halt one after another in the sandy mud, before being wrenched free to lie beside the useless vehicles. It was too late, the men were trapped: too far to reach the shore where their prey was now safely encamped, too far to return in safety - and those mountainous waves were constantly threatening. Then the frightened soldiers, innate trepidation rising to the surface, did the unthinkable. They not only broke ranks, but openly opposed Pharaoh, even disobeying him. As one man, they shouted to each other, 'Let us flee from the face of Israel, for the Lord fighteth for them against the Egyptians' (Exod. 14:25). It was not a sentiment likely to be appreciated back in the Egyptian court had they returned home, but it was the heart cry of surrender from desperate men.

And did these frightened soldiers care for the sweating panic-stricken horses rearing and struggling between the shafts, or galloping off dragging the broken chariots through the mud? Probably not, they ran or rather slithered back the way they had come, and how long it was taking! Would the waters maintain their present position?

Surely not for long, and their dark shadows chilled hearts still further. And even if they saw the bank towards which they were struggling, how far yet to go! Perhaps they knew, but hope had gone.

They little realised their struggles were being watched by the Lord of both heaven and earth (Matt.11:25), the One who had determined their end (Exod.14:24). His chief opponent was Pharaoh (Rom.9:17), but the King's men were as idolatrous as he and Jehovah's vengeance was inevitable (Is.42:8). Thus, at a given moment the restraint released, the Creator caused the two halves of his sea to roll together crushingly.

He could have done it without reference to Moses, but his servant's authority had to be witnessed by the nation as a whole. Sympathy was in short supply as Moses stretched out his hand over the sea once more (Exod.14:26,27), the honour and glory of God far outweighing the comfort and safety of his creatures.

The only mercy offered to Pharaoh and hundreds of his men (Ps.136:15), at least as far as this world was concerned, was that the end was swift: 'there remained not so much as one of them' (Exod.14:28). Without warning, the walls of water on each side of the struggling men and horses suddenly descended with a thunderous roar (Jer.49:21) like the voice of 'terrible things' (Ps. 106:22; Rev.1:15). The event was a great leveller, as the King was swirled to the depths with the commoners; the humans with the animals (Exod.15:1), before permitting their bloated bodies to rise to the surface to float with what remained of the chariots.

DRAWN TO THE MOUNT

Having experienced the sovereign power of God to such a remarkable degree, not only during the time in Egypt (Exod.7-12), but particularly now after the astonishing miracle they had just witnessed, a stunned silence must surely have settled upon the Hebrews. The sight of hundreds of corpses floating in the sea, and lying on the shore, merely served to underline the greatness of what Jehovah had accomplished, and also the depth of his love for them. Truly, he had showed them 'his glory and his greatness' (Deut.5:24).

But astonishment quickly turned to euphoria, incredulity to national rejoicing, in the realisation that freedom from slavery had finally been achieved. But having stared back across the sea at what remained of Egyptian pride, the Hebrews then fixed their minds upon the God of their salvation. The entire experience was even recorded in song ('Moses' song') for he led the singing, while the women joined his sister Miriam in musical gaiety and festive dancing. 'Sing ye to the Lord', was the cry, 'for he hath triumphed gloriously' (Exod.15). After a lifetime of slavery, and pleadings to Jehovah for his help (Exod.2:23), the largest of burdens had rolled away, carried to freedom on 'eagles' wings' (Exod.19:4). They did not know it, but their exultation symbolised much greater rejoicing that would be experienced, and everlastingly, by another 'holy nation' chosen by their God (Rev.15:3).

But the festivities drew to an inevitable end, the music and the dancing trailing away into the desert dust, practical realities having to be confronted. A mere three days into their journey, they who had just been rejoicing in God's saving power, were already questioning his keeping powers (1 Peter 1:5). 'We're free!' had quickly been substituted by 'We're thirsty!' (Exod.15:24) and 'We're hungry!' (Exod.16:3), and such was the astonishing fickleness of the peoples' character, Egypt was preferred. And this was only day three of what was destined to be wilderness wanderings lasting forty years (Numb.14:34)! It was just as well the nation did not know it at the time.

But the panic was as needless as faith could have told them; intelligence too, for would God have accomplished so much for his people just to desert them on Egypt's doorstep (Exod.7-14)? Would he have intervened miraculously on their behalf without sound reasons behind it? On the other hand, perhaps there was some point to their fears. Had not Moses requested Pharaoh that he should release the slaves for a three day trip into the desert for religious purposes (Exod.3:18; 5:3)? The three days were now up (Exod.15:22)!

His peoples' petulance though – so grievous, an area was appropriately named to mark the spot (Exod.17:7) - did not discourage Jehovah from encouraging THEM. The miraculous was not in short supply. As Moses later learned he is 'longsuffering, and abundant in goodness' (Exod.34:6). Miracles are always unexpected and filled with surprises, thus although isolated in a desert region, in no time food was plucked from the air each evening, and 'the corn' or 'the bread of heaven' (Pss. 78:24; 105:40) picked from the ground ('angel's food', Ps.78:25) first thing six mornings out of seven, and on the sixth enough for the Sabbath too (Exodus 16:22). Also a plentiful supply of water gushed from a rock struck by Moses at God's command (Exod.16-17; Neh.9:15; Ps.78:15). Pharaoh's former slaves were unaware of it, but the generous provision miraculously supplied symbolised the spiritual sustenance Satan's former slaves would one day receive (John 6:31-35; 7:37,38).

Two full months passed since their departure from Egypt, eight eventful weeks in which murmuring and the miraculous were coupled together. There was even a war, won by a sovereign God and a prayerful Moses, an unforgettable skirmish with marauding Amalekites (a people finally dealt with by Solomon's father many years later, 2 Sam.8:11,12) taking advantage of the vulnerable Hebrews (Exod.17: 8-16; Numb.24:20).

Then one day a mountain range came into view, dominating the skyline, whose highest peak is 8,000 feet above sea level; the pillar of cloud had brought them to Sinai, situated at the apex of a peninsula whose shape is that of a vast triangle 260 miles long and 150 miles wide at the northern end. After many weeks of trudging through the flat and arid desert, this impressive sight must have been a refreshing change, particularly when the order was issued to set up the encampment at the foot of its cooling shades.

What activity there was as the 2,000,000, or thereabouts (Exod.12:37), settled in to their new environment that first evening: belongings unpacked, tents erected, herds and flocks penned, the children controlled, the elderly cared for, and a welcomed meal prepared. With Sinai looming large over them, here they were to remain for a year (Exod.19:1; Numb.1:1), during which time more about that 'Name' so fascinating to Sheba would be revealed.

Then shortly after their arrival, with a measured step a solitary figure, staff in hand, was seen slowly ascending the mount. Many would have watched him until he could be seen no more, and

wondered what surprises Moses had in store for them this time
(Exod.19:3). They soon discovered.

How long he was away is uncertain, within hours (Exod.19:
10), but when he returned he had a message from God to impart
(Exod.19:4-6), that would have been of special interest to Sheba
because it referred to the covenant he had made with Abraham
(Gen.12:1-3). He had brought them safely from Egypt to this spot
('I bare you on eagles' wings'), and now obedience to the covenant
was demanded, that which God expects of those he is pleased to
love and call his 'peculiar treasure', a holy nation (Exod.19:5; 1
Peter 2:9) and 'a kingdom of priests' (Rev.1:6). With her pagan
background in mind she would also have noted the reference to the
earth belonging solely to him.

That day the people made it known to Moses, probably through
the elders of the nation, that a vow had been made. They would
indeed obey God, and this fact was taken back to him (Exod.19:7,8).
When Moses returned once more it was with exciting, if not alarming,
news. The One before whom they had made that vow, their Creator
and Deliverer (Exod.6:7), was shortly to make his appearance before
them all (Exod.19:9-13).

But what did that mean? The people had no idea, a fact that
instilled an even greater fear within the nation. If Moses had been
capable of confounding their enemies, bringing destruction in its
wake (Exod.7-14), how much more fearful much he be who provided
Moses with the means to create such havoc. What would happen
when he came? What would he look like? What would he do?

For the next two days they were given a glimpse of what was
about to occur, when preparation was made for the remarkable
occasion. Each tent was transformed into a hive of activity, as
cleanliness was shown to be next to godliness, each article of clothing
having to be washed (Exod.19:10,14). How soiled it must have been
after eight weeks travelling through the dust of the desert, but the
scrubbing and the washing by the women (presumably) was not for
practical reasons, but rather the reminder of the purity of the One
they were to meet (Lev.11:44).

The men were equally active. They were called upon to erect
fencing at the base of the mount in order to restrain both animals

and humans from venturing beyond it, the warning given by God through his servant to 'take heed'. Even the base of Sinai had not to be touched, and should that happen 'he shall surely be stoned, or shot through, whether it be beast or man' (Exod.19:13). The perfect purity of the Divine is never something to trifle with and fallen mankind, fallen nature too, has constantly to be made aware of that fact (Gen.3). God is 'holy, harmless, undefiled, separate from sinners, and made higher than the heavens' (Heb.7:26).

There were then two further commands issued that probably surprised the people. First, celibacy during those two days of preparation was ordered, because with the immanent appearance of the Almighty the soul had to prevail over the flesh, meditation over copulation (Exod.19:15). Secondly, the people were to expect the heralding of the Manifestation, the blast of a 'trumpet', at which point they were to proceed to the foot of the mount (Exod.19:13). With that expectation they retired to their tents at the close of the second day, feelings decidedly mixed: excitement, dread, and fear being uppermost. Few could have slept that night.

NINE
Blood, Oil and Fire

The night had been sleepless and dawn arrived far too slowly, but when at last it edged its way over the horizon, it would have found the Hebrews waiting. Jehovah, their unseen benefactor when desperation had reached its peak (Exod.2:23), was about to appear. Mount Sinai, rearing up in front of them, was the chosen venue (Exod.19:11). Who could have remained inside his tent that morning?

One of the many things they had learned, that walking with God is a great adventure, the surprises are many and often. One moment they were slaves, the next victors; one moment crying to him for help, the next recipients of his rescue plan; one moment unbelieving, the next carried along on the waves of the miraculous; one moment despondent, the next heartened. And all this in so short a time. Thus thoughts were plentiful, fears too. From the most important to the least (Exod.18:25), from the sage to the simpleton, the aged to the youth: all wondered what was likely to happen, and when. All eyes were towards Sinai, where else were they likely to be on such a day?

They were not to wait long. Soon Moses ordered the elders of the nation - the 'rulers of thousands, rulers of hundreds, rulers of fifties, and rulers of tens (Exod.18:25)' – to assemble the people, an action not easy to carry out. Freed slaves enjoying their freedom, and so many of them, were likely to be undisciplined and unwilling to receive commands again. The fact that they were under control revealed the impact made upon them by the presence of God, and the strength of Moses' character. He now led them, this 'kingdom of priests' (Exod.19:6; 1 Peter 2:9), to the foot of the mount.

The sky was cloudless, yet suddenly anger flared in the firmament as God 'declared his strength' among the people (Ps. 77:14). The expectant atmosphere was rocked by rumbling as continuous thunder rolled angrily overhead (Ps.29:3), 'blackness, and darkness, and tempest' (Heb.12:18). Sinners were present, and heaven's 'rebuke' could be the only response (Ps.104:7). Then, again without warning, jagged lightning streaked towards the mount, immediately followed without respite by other fearsome flashes. Eyes were shielded and the observers wanted to 'haste away' in their fearfulness (Ps.104:7), but naked power unleashed from heaven discounts all such attempts; a foretaste of things to come (Matt.24:27), and as terrifying (2 Thess.1:8).

By this time, Sinai was the scene of an even greater and more extraordinary phenomenon. A dense cloud engulfed the mount (Exod.19:16), bright with radiance as myriads of angels heralded Jehovah's presence (Deut.33:2; Heb.12:22), and from its heart the blast of a 'trumpet' long and loud resounded over the people of God (Exod.19:16), who pleaded for it to cease (Heb.12: 19), for no one can speak louder than God Almighty (Rev.1:10).

The mighty Sinai appeared to 'melt' under the weight of the glory (Judg.5:5). The appointed time of visitation had arrived, and they were being summoned to appear before their Sovereign Lord (1 Thess.2:16,17). In only a brief period they had been transformed from slaves to sons; had been transported from the mundane to the miraculous. It was a 'holy place' indeed (Ps.68:17; Heb.12:22), and one that is due to reappear at the close of the age (Matt.24:30,31; Jude 14).

The nation trembled, and watched as Moses slowly approached the mount 'beckoned' by the voice of God. To the peoples' alarm he crossed the barrier recently erected to restrain them, and beneath the awesome canopy of heaven's angry voice (Ps.18:13), he gradually ascended the steep incline. They watched him walking further from them, his noble figure getting smaller with each step, until the cloud enveloped him and he was lost from their sight. What they did not know was that, although a great man accustomed to meeting with God, he was as terrified as they were (Heb.12:21).

He had need to be, as much as the people he led, because the greatest lesson mankind as a whole learned that day was how unapproachable is God, the pathway to him being paved with perfect purity (1 Tim.6:16); the light of holiness reflecting divine wrath against sin (1 John 1:5), as Moses was learning the hard way as he approached God through the immense storm; something he had quickly discovered upon first meeting with him (Exod.3:5).

And it was Jehovah himself who supplied the remedy to mankind's tragic dilemma, when he appointed someone to mediate between himself and sinners, one who would soon be wearing the insignia of his new office, 'HOLINESS TO THE LORD' (Exod. 28:36): entitled 'high priest', both one with God and at the same time associated with sinners. Who could fulfil such an office? On the mount that fearful moment God revealed to Moses who it would be. No one dared even touch the mount, sanctified as it was by the divine presence, including the priestly elders, but in the future Moses could approach God 'thou, and AARON with thee' (Exod.19:12,24); not necessarily always literally walking beside him (Exod.24:14; 32:1), but at least functioning as high priest within the nation (Lev.8).

TWO FURTHER QUESTIONS

But this teaching would have provoked an intelligent person to enquire still further. First of all, what is 'sin'? The concept of 'sin' would have differed sharply from that recognised by Solomon and his people, one understood only when measured by its antithesis; for the Queen of the South, that would be behaviour unacceptable to the ruling body, to the majority in the community, or to both.

No doubt the kingdom over which the Queen ruled was governed well, an official eye fixed upon the way her subjects behaved, with stern punishments for 'sinners' who failed the 'acceptable' standards. But they could reach no higher than that; certainly not to their gods, who merely mirrored the moral aspirations of their adherents. An idol has eyes, ears and a mouth, but the worshippers can do as they please (Ps.115:5-8) – even within centimetres of its 'gaze' (Jer.10:5).

But then Sheba journeyed to Israel and learned a disturbing concept she had not known before: holiness, and reflected in white light, the grotesque nature of sin. Not 'sin' as she would have recognised it, that which incurred the displeasure of those in authority, but rather sin as an enemy of the mighty God of Israel; sin in its ugliness exposed against the backcloth of 'the perfection of beauty' (Ps.50:2). That attractive quality, by which suggested Solomon's father Jehovah must be worshipped (Ps.29:2), was surely an aspect of the wisdom for which Solomon was famous, and the quality Sheba must have been aware of when she first set eyes upon him.

For someone with her background to be taught about the perfect righteousness of God must have been alarming for her, particularly when her conscience confronted the application of that truth as it must surely have done. After all, did not the echoes of David's grief over his sin with Bathsheba and against her husband Uriah still reverberate around the royal household (2 Sam.11)? There were those of Solomon's court who would have remembered David's distress when the child he had by Bathsheba died (2 Sam. 12:15-23). And also observed in his demeanour the result of his soul's agony as a result of his sin: 'I acknowledge my transgressions, and my sin is ever before me. Against thee, thee only, have I sinned, and done this evil in thy sight...' Sheba would also have learned the truth from Solomon, as he had learned it from his father, that she too was 'shapen in iniquity', and 'in sin' had her mother conceived her (Ps.51:3-5).

But what exactly IS sin? It would have been this question (and there was no other way to explain the existence of the temple, and its predecessor the tabernacle) that had provoked Solomon into relating the account about Moses' descent from Sinai with God's Law in his hands. No guest of his could have avoided hearing the story, particularly in relation to temple worship (1 Kings 8:50).

God having revealed the perfection of his character - and also his antipathy towards the imperfections of his human creatures, whom at the beginning he had driven from his presence because of their disobedience (Gen.2:16,17; 3:24) - placed on record the duties he demands of every individual from fallen mankind: the moral law, the ten commandments, written on tablets of stone (Exod.20:1-17; 34:29). They number so few as to be treated superficially by the unthinking, yet each one is a mirror to the soul that no conscience can look into without smarting.

Sheba could not have been an exception. She would have noted they are easily divided into two sections; one to four, duties towards God (Exod.20:3-11), and five to ten, duties towards one's neighbour (Exod.20:12-17). That is: accepting the uniqueness of Israel's God (Deut.6:4), refusing to recognize another deity (Is.42: 8), observing due reverence towards him (Lev.19:12), and remembering his creative power (Gen.2:2) and disciplining one's life accordingly (Exod.20:10,11). Just the first four in the moral law, and Sheba had been breaking all of them throughout her life!

Then again, had she honoured her father and mother, and all of the time, without wavering (Lev.19:3)? Had she never killed anyone (Prov.10:12), not even in her heart (Matt.5:21,22), or taken another woman's husband (Prov.9:13-15)? Had she ever stolen anything? Nothing? But having served idols, what about the robbing of the glory due to Jehovah? Perhaps her neighbours had never been slandered from behind her hand, or that which was rightfully theirs coveted? She would surely have blushed.

In other words with every other member of the human race, whether a palace was their home or a hovel, Sheba was confronted with heaven's command: 'thou shalt love the Lord thy God with all thine heart, and with all thy soul, and with all thy might' (Deut.6:5; Matt.22:37). She had not done so, and therefore had broken God's holy law, and THAT is what he considers sin to be (1 John 3:4). It was a far cry from what Sheba had experienced before, and whether she hung her head or not in shame is unknown (Rom.7: 23,24), but to know of one's awful plight before God is better than being left in complete darkness. It was another good reason for a worthwhile journey.

Now, she understood why there was a need for Aaron the high priest to have the names of the Israelite tribes inscribed on the precious stones within his 'breastplate of judgment', and also on his shoulders (Exod.28:9-36). He was the mediator between God and sinners, representing God to the people, and the people to God.

But intelligence could not be completely satisfied with that explanation, there being something incomplete about it. Aaron was a sinful man (as events illustrated, Exod.32) and was therefore qualified to represent his equally sinful contemporaries, but what credentials did he possess to represent God to them; likewise, Azariah the high priest known to Solomon (1 Kings 4:2), to whom Sheba had probably been introduced? Unless of course these two men, and their successors, represented someone else; Someone who was like God, and like man, at the same time (1 Tim.2:5; Heb. 4:14-16).

Were Aaron and Azariah only 'shadows' of heavenly things (Heb.10:1)? It would have appeared likely to a serious enquirer. Certainly Solomon's father was in possession of a vision, of One seated at the Lord's right hand (Ps.110:1; Acts 2:34; Heb.12:2); of the Lord being both before him (as man) as well as at his side (as God) (Ps.16:8). The 'name' was taking shape in Sheba's mind; a mysterious Figure would one day appear, die a Victim upon an 'altar' as a substitute for others (Gen.22), for sinners (Exod.20:1-17), and yet according to David's vision would also be seated beside God (Ps.100:1). Was this 'Someone', Sheba might have asked, Abraham's Visitor (Gen.12:1) and Moses' Angel (Exod.3:1-5)?

PRIESTS AND LEVITES

No admirer of the temple, as every foreign guest in Solomon's palace would have been, could escape noticing the priests whose work revolved around it. Asking questions about the one would entail discovering answers about the other.

Sheba would have learned that the Israelite priesthood had been instituted at the time when Aaron and his four sons had been chosen as the first priests (Exod.28:1). That is, shortly after the day Moses descended mount Sinai with the Law written upon the stone tablets in his arms (Exod.34:29).

They were not chosen arbitrarily, but with the purposes of God in mind. The father of Moses, Aaron and Miriam was a man called Levi (Exod.6:16), and he was divinely selected as the pro-genitor of the Levitical priesthood. In the early days at least, the high priest could only have been the eldest son of a direct descendant of Levi.

But Levi had three other sons, Gershon, Kohath and Merari, and from these were descended the Levites, whose role was practical rather than sacrificial. The work of both priests and Levites was difficult, in fact a five year apprenticeship was served, from twenty-five years old to thirty, culminating in an early retirement at the age of fifty (Numb.4:23; 8:24-26). David lowered the age of commencement to twenty, a ruling that continued after the Exile (1 Chron.23:24,27), although Jesus fulfilled the original law commencing his ministry at 'about thirty years of age' (Matt.5: 17; Luke 3:23).

If the function of the priests was self-explanatory, that of the 22,300 male Levites was less so, although they were as dedicated to the tabernacle as the priests, and encamped just behind it: the 7,500 Gershonites to the west, the 8,600 Kohathites to the south, and the 6,200 of Merari to the north (Numb.3:22-35). Each family of Levites was given its own tasks to perform. Throughout the forty years of the desert wanderings (Numb.14:33), the tabernacle repeatedly erected and then dismantled as the nation moved steadily onwards guided by the pillar of cloud (Exod.40:36), the Levites went about their work.

While the Gershonites were responsible for the fabrics of the tabernacle, carried in two wagons pulled by four oxen (Numb.4:24-28; 7:7), the men of Merari dealt with the boards, pillars and sockets, which they stacked in four separate wagons pulled by eight oxen (Numb.4:29-33; 7;8). In the meantime the Kohathites had a special function, and a more difficult one, because their duty was to carry on their shoulders the covenantal ark, the holy vessels and the tabernacle furniture. That is, objects made of wood and gold. Small wonder they were obliged to retire when they had reached fifty years of age (Numb.8:25)! They always arrived at the scene later than the other Levites, because what they carried had first to be covered by

Aaron and his priestly sons (Numb.4:5) for no eye dared see the sacred objects (Numb.4: 4-20).

THE TENT OF THE CONGREGATION

In contrast to the ornate temple, the tabernacle was of a simple and intensely practical design, suitable for mobility in desert regions. Not surprisingly, the idea behind its existence as well as the 'blueprint' originated from God (Exod.25:9), who was laying down the principles for worship acceptable to him.

The 'tent of the congregation', as it was called, was just that, a tent (Exod.40:34), made up of fourteen different kinds of material, and covered fourfold. The first covering formed the ceiling, multi-coloured carpeting (purple, scarlet, blue and the purest white) and embroidered with cherubim. Aaron and his fellow priests only had to lift their heads to be reminded of the business in which they were engaged. Then lying on top of it were two more layers, the skins of rams (dyed red) and 'badgers' (conies, Ps.104:18), and finally the top-most covering was a carpeting of goats' hair that had been especially spun by the Israelite women (Exod.26:7,14; 35:26).

Holding it all in place were boards of gold-covered acacia wood each one resting on a base of silver (Exod.26:15-29); silver which came from the Israelites' 'ransom money' of half a shekel a person (Exod.30:11-16; 38:25-27). These boards were connected on the outside by four poles that ran through gold rings. The poles were also made from acacia wood and gold-covered.

The walls of the tent were comprised of ten curtains, divided into two panels of five curtains each, twenty eight cubits long and held together by fifty golden clasps each end of which was inserted in one of the fifty blue loops (Exod.26:1-6). The curtains displayed the standard multi colours of purple, scarlet, blue and white.

Surrounding the tabernacle was a courtyard one hundred cubits long and fifty wide, bordered by walls of the finest fibre (white byssus) hung from pillars made of acacia wood, overlaid at the top by silver and at the base by brass. There were sixty of them connected to each other by silver rods, twenty at its length, and ten at its width.

Entrance into the courtyard was through a 'gate' twenty cubits wide, a curtain familiarly multi-coloured (Exod.27: 9-18).

The tabernacle, like the temple it foreshadowed as mentioned earlier (Chapter seven), was divided into two sections, the holy place and the most holy place. The interior of the former, which only the priests were permitted to enter (Exod.27:21), was hidden from view by another multi-coloured curtain, supported by five pillars made of acacia wood, the tops of which were gold. Each pillar rested upon a brass base (Exod.26:36,37).

The latter, the most holy place (like the heavenly city, Rev. 21:16, cube-shaped, all of its dimensions being ten cubits) was also hidden from view this time from all the priests except one. Only the high priest was permitted to enter (apart from having to cover the ark of the covenant each time the tabernacle was dismantled when the nation moved on, Exod.40:36), and that annually on the most important day in the Israelite calendar, the great day of atonement (Exod.28:12; Lev.16; Heb.9:7).

A heavy dividing multi-coloured curtain like the others, suspended from golden hooks and supported by four pillars made as one would by now expect from acacia wood and resting upon silver, separated the two sections (Exod.26:33). Embroidered on this 'veil' were cherubim, symbolic heavenly figures 'guarding' the holiest of all (Heb.9:3), as in reality cherubim with swords of flame protected the tree of life in the Garden of Eden (Gen.3:24).

The Israelite's ideal number was seven (Gen.1:31), and perhaps it was not a coincidence that the tabernacle (as well as the temple) consisted of the seven basic items as mentioned already (Chapter seven): the altar of burnt offering and the brazen laver in the courtyard; the seven-branched candlestick, the table upon which was bread, and the altar of incense within the holy place; the covenantal ark and its 'mercy seat' overshadowed by golden cherubim beyond the veil in the most holy place (Exod.25; Heb.9: 1-5).

The skins of rams and badgers, and the hair of goats, these were easily acquired, but where would the former slaves have got hold of gold, silver, brass, wood, jewels, the fabrics for making the curtains, and the robes for the priests? The answer lay in the provision Jehovah made for his people, making sure their enemies supplied their every need (Exod.3:21,22). Having witnessed the country's devastation (Exod.10:7), the Egyptians were only too pleased to rid themselves of the Israelites, and thus as they departed from 'the land of Ham' (Ps.105:23), to their undoubted astonishment the descendants of Shem (Gen.10:21) discovered they were given exactly what they wanted (Exod.12:31-36).

And what expertise was required in erecting the tabernacle, a meticulous attention to detail, and in so many practical areas: carpentry, joinery, metallography, embroidery, tailoring, dyeing, and more besides! If the sufferings of the Israelites had united them in prayer (Exod.2:23), the requirements of the tabernacle united them in practical matters also.

Jehovah had exercised his sovereign power in rescuing them from Egypt, but freedom now demanded a response on their part. They were to give freely of their time, possessions and talents towards the establishing of the sanctuary and everything that pertained to it (Exod.25:2). The more practically minded among the people volunteered their services to work (Exod.28:3): carrying and chopping, designing and dyeing, sawing and sewing. Overall were two supervisors especially gifted by God, Bezaleel and Aholiab (Exod.36:1; 37:1).

And thus after a year encamped at Sinai, the tabernacle was erected (Exod.19:1; 40:17,33), the incandescent cloud of glory enveloped it, and to such a degree even Moses was unable to enter. He had been caught up in this unique cloud before, but not on this occasion. The intensity of God's nearness was too profound (Exod.19:20; 40:35). At the inauguration of temple worship something similar was experienced, as Solomon no doubt informed Sheba, when the priests were overcome by the manifestation of the heavenly grace (1 Kings 8:10,11).

PREPARATION FOR SERVICE

One vital ingredient though was missing. But first, those for whom the sanctuary would from now on be central throughout the remainder of their lives were publicly committed to their roles before the entire nation (Lev.8:1-3). It was a most solemn occasion, as Moses' brother and his four nephews received heaven's approval: anointed, consecrated and sanctified (Exod.28:41) as the first members of the newly established 'royal priesthood' (1 Peter 2:9; Rev.1:6).

From each quarter of the encampment they came, the men, the women and the children, assembling at the entrance to the courtyard of the sanctuary. The rays of the sun shining upon the tabernacle highlighted its pristine condition: the white courtyard walls sparkling, the brass of the altar glistening, the water in the laver shimmering, and the mirrors from which it was constructed flashing (Exod.38:8).

So many were present few could have seen what took place within that forbidden area, but to have mingled in the multitude was sufficient blessing, as the words of Moses had been made known to them all: 'This is the thing which the Lord commanded to be done. (Lev.8:5)'

Watched by the people whom they were to serve, Aaron and his sons accompanied Moses (and presumably an assistant or two) to the place most needed at that moment: the laver (Exod.29:4; 40: 12; Lev.8:6), the tabernacle possessing just one-tenth of the 'seas' in the temple (1 Kings 7:38)! Here in water God had earlier supplied miraculously (Exod.17:6), the priestly family was washed. From then on, the laver would be used before entering the holy place each time (Exod.30:19-21). It was a symbolic gesture, because the 'waters' of sanctification are essential for those who dare to serve heaven (Titus 3:5).

Aaron took precedence, and the ceremonial washing over, his brother assisted him in his enrobing for the great high priest's office, and as one has come to expect in an examination of Israelite practices (Gen.2:2), SEVEN special articles of clothing were to adorn him 'for glory and for beauty', each one with a significance to underline (Exod.28:1-39).

First the white cotton undercoat and its matching belt for purity (Heb.7:26), then the robe coloured with the blue of heaven, its hem lined with tiny golden bells and pomegranates (Exod.28: 33-35); the embroidered ephod (1 Sam.2:28), an outer garment reaching almost to the knees, threaded with beaten gold and woven in purple, scarlet and blue the colours associated with the sanctuary (Exod.26:31), with two large gems fastened to each shoulder, upon which were engraved the names of six Israelite tribes apiece (Exod.28:9-12); the ephod's belt of identical design, through which everyday attire was sanctified, as well as the divine condescension in elevating the elect to the priesthood (John 13:4,5; Rev.1:13); the square breastplate mentioned above, of the same design and material as the ephod (Exod.28:22-28), decorated with the twelve precious jewels set in gold (Exod.28:15-21), and finally the headgear, white for purity, fronted with 'HOLINESS TO THE LORD' (Exod.28:36-38) engraved upon a golden plaque (Lev.8:6-9).

THE OIL FOR ANOINTING

Did Solomon introduce his royal guest to these intricate matters related to the tabernacle? Perhaps not had she been an ordinary visitor to his kingdom, but her appearance in Jerusalem was far from ordinary; her quest and curiosity demanded a discussion about the temple and its forerunner. Questions about the Lord's 'name' is bound up with the subject (Phil.2:9,10).

But water was not the only element used on the occasion of the priesthood's inauguration. Sheba would not have been surprised to learn that oil featured too, a commodity whose use was widespread in ancient times, and no doubt in her country also, particularly on festive occasions.

Israel flowed with oil; olive trees were in abundance. A famous Mount illustrated the fact (2 Sam.15:30; Matt.26:30). Unripe olives gathered by hand, or gently shaken from the trees, produced the best quality (Job 15:33). Oil from the olive was used domestically, its failure at harvest time signifying famine (Hab.3: 17), and on one occasion was exported for political reasons to Egypt as a bribe to a Pharaoh (Hos.12:1).

It was golden in colour (Zech.4:12), referred to as 'pure oil olive beaten', and was used to light the seven-branched candlestick in the holy place (Exod.25:6; 27:20). Also, for the Israelites oil-anointing was expressive of joy (Pss.23:5; 92:10), or just general well-being (Ruth 3:3; Ps.104:15); fasting too (Matt:6:17). The omission of the anointing signified sorrow (2 Sam.14:2).

There was, however, one aspect of its use that Sheba would probably not have known about before her visit to Jerusalem; the fact that anointing with oil, when mixed with certain ingredients, was expressive of a sacred moment. Could Solomon have refrained from relating the account of that special day when his father was a youth, and the mighty Samuel had visited his home in order to choose the future king of Israel? Surely not, it was one of the most momentous occasions in the nation's history, when before the great prophet the young man knelt to receive the anointing, and in doing so 'the Spirit of the Lord came upon David from that day forward' (1 Sam.16:4-13).

Like so much else in Israelite tradition, oil-anointing as a sacred act had its roots in the history of the patriarchs. While asleep under a starry sky Jacob had a dream. He saw a ladder reaching to heaven upon which were angels ascending and descending (John 1:43-51). It was the occasion when the covenant God had made with Abraham was ratified to Jacob his grandson (Gen.28:10-15): 'I am the God of Abraham, the God of Isaac', and now, 'the God of Jacob' (Exod.3:6).

When Jacob awoke realising the importance and sacredness of what had happened, he called the place 'Beth-el' because 'this is none other but the house of God, and this is the gate of heaven'. Jacob made a memorial of the stone he had used as a pillow and anointed it with oil, and in doing so 'vowed a vow' (Gen.28:16-22; 31:13). From then on in the Israelite story sacred moments were marked with the anointing of oil, the symbol of a covenantal transaction between God and his people.

Thus having enrobed Aaron in the sight of heaven and the entire nation, Moses solemnly anointed the tabernacle and everything that would be involved in the worship of almighty God. This included his brother as the first temporal high priest (Ps.133: 1,2), and once he had enrobed them, his four priestly nephews to: Nadab, Abihu, Eleazar and Ithamar (Exod.28:1,41; Lev.8:10-13).

THE BLOOD FOR ATONEMENT

But the anointing was not limited to the use of oil. Blood also featured prominently, animal blood, that of a bullock and two rams

(Lev.8:14,18,22), the latter stirring memories in Sheba of what occurred on the temple mount in Abraham's day (Gen.22:13).

Then something unusual happened. Moses walked the few yards from the laver to the altar, dipped his finger in the bowl of the bullock's blood and smeared the 'horns' that were fixed to each corner (Exod.29:10-14): that is, the knobs to which the cords binding the sacrifice would be tied (Ps.118:27), as Isaac had been bound on Abraham's makeshift altar (Gen.22:9). Then Moses poured the blood around the base of the altar, in this way 'sanctifying' it (Heb.9:21). Then portions of the bullock's carcase were burned; the 'waste products' disposed of outside the camp, but the animal's vital organs, the most significant and symbolic parts, were offered up on the altar (Lev.8:16,17).

The first ram was then produced (Exod.29:15-18). As with the bullock, so with the ram; Aaron and his sons laid their hands upon it in recognition of the substitutionary element in the procedure, their identification with what was shortly to take place (Lev.8:14,18). Slaughtered, the ram's blood was also sprinkled over and around the altar, before its carcase was burned upon it as a sacrificial offering (Lev.8:18-21).

Then the second ram, 'the ram of consecration', was brought to the scene (Exod.29:19-21). Again, the hands of the newly formed priesthood were laid upon it before it also surrendered to the knife. But now something even stranger took place. Once more blood was used as a 'sanctifying' agency, but before the altar was doused in it Moses placed some on Aaron and his sons: the tip of the right ear, the thumb of the right hand, and the big toe of the right foot (Lev.8:23,24).

At that point, though, the mystery was still by no means unravelled. With the dexterity of a butcher, Moses dissected the carcase according to the command of God (Exod.29:22,23), and reached for a bread basket prepared for the occasion (Lev.8:26). From it he took an unleavened cake, a cake of oiled bread, and a wafer, which he placed on the separated fatty tissue of this 'ram of consecration'.

The strange ingredient was then placed on Aaron and his four sons' outstretched hands (before being offered up in fire upon the altar, Exod.29:25), ready to be 'waved' before God: that is, the hands gently moving from side to side, as the men looked towards the tabernacle in which was the ark of the covenant secreted within the most holy place (Exod.25:22). That having been accomplished, Moses 'sanctified' his brother and his nephews by sprinkling the anointing oil and the blood upon them and their priestly robes (Lev.8:30). There was much else besides, on an occasion of intricate detail. What did it all mean?

It concerned the use made of one of the most vital components of the body, whether human or animal: blood. Without it there is no life (Lev.17:11,14). It is therefore precious to man, but even more so to God who created it, as every Semitic race believed (Gen.9:4-6; Acts 15:20), including that to which Sheba belonged (Gen.25:1-3). She would therefore have had at least a partial understanding of what transpired that day within the courtyard of the tabernacle; the shedding of blood, even that of the animals, was a sacred act performed in the presence of deity.

But as blood flowing in the veins signified life (Lev.17:11), to the Semitic mind the word 'blood' could also signify death (Rev. 19:13). For example, in telling the Amalekite who had killed Saul that his intended execution was his own fault, David said, 'Thy blood be upon thy head' (2 Sam.1:16). And when lives were risked obtaining water for him (2 Sam.23:15-17), he refused to drink it: 'Shall I drink the blood of these men...? (1 Chron.11:17-19). Or again, one hears his heartfelt prayer: 'What profit is there in my blood, when I go down to the pit (Ps.30:9)?'

The shedding of blood though was not considered just the cessation of life, but death brought about by violence (Acts 5:28). Hence, the Lord's accusation after Cain had murdered Abel: 'the voice of thy brother's blood crieth unto me from the ground' (Gen. 4:10). Likewise, Jacob's expressed fear when he saw his son's coat covered in blood: 'An evil beast hath devoured him; Joseph is without doubt rent in pieces'. Joseph's brothers knew their father would react in that way, 'without doubt' was his son killed, when they dipped the coat in blood (Gen.37:31-33).

God himself took the concept a stage further. He revealed that this precious commodity of blood, the symbol of death by violence, was the means to bring about reconciliation between himself and the sinner: 'it is the blood that maketh an atonement ('at-one-ment') for the soul' (Lev.17:11). Clearly, there was to be no other way to appease the God of perfect righteousness; without blood-shedding sin would remain, and divine judgment exercised (Heb.9:22).

The nation already had cause to heed the warning at the first 'pass-over', the night it was rescued from Egypt. The people were commanded to 'strike the lintel and the two side posts with the blood' of a lamb, because, said God, 'when I see the blood, I will pass over you'. As a result, as noted earlier, judgment from the 'destroyer' was averted (Exod.12:13-23).

But these are difficult lessons to learn, even alarming to every beginner like Sheba, that the salvation of a soul involves so much violence and bloodshed. Why should that be? Could not God have devised a 'smoother' pathway to heaven, paved perhaps with the perfumed spices like those she had brought from Marib (1 Kings 10:2)? Sinners would love to have it so, for they refuse to acknowledge their soul's condition, or their plight before God. To touch but the 'hem' of understanding about Atoning Sacrifice, the student has first to grapple with this dilemma.

To begin with, there is something terribly twisted about human beings: loving and lustful, liking and loathing, selfless and selfish, generous and greedy. What a maze of complexities, tightly entwined with so many paradoxes! It is due to mankind's fall from the Creator's favour (Gen.3:24).

Until that moment Adam and Eve had enjoyed sweet fellowship with him in the Garden of Eden, a loving and peaceful union (Ps.8:5). They were free, although within the framework of love. But that freedom was soon to be tested. Satan (Lucifer), who had sought to deify himself, caused a rebellion in heaven and was banished from God's presence (Is.14:12-15) together with the angels who supported him (Jude 6). He arrived in Eden.

God had warned the 'first parents' that 'death' would be the outcome of disobedience (Gen.2:17), the cessation of both physical and spiritual life (1 Cor.15:22), experiences unknown until that time. By encouraging Eve to mistrust God's Word, she fell into the trap Satan had laid for her, and in turn persuaded Adam to follow her example (Gen.3:1-6). The result was that sin entered the world - 'death reigned' (Rom.5:14,21) – and fellowship was broken (Gen.3:24). Mankind as a whole was out in the cold.

The fall was so profound, the consequences so dire, the experience has never been fully understood or appreciated by the majority, and consequently neither have the purposes of God in redemption. The state of 'death' is not that of unconsciousness, it is the complete absence of life. In Adam (Rom.5:17; 1 Cor.15:22), from the moment of conception a human creature is physically dying and spiritually dead (Ephes.2:1; Col.2:13). Put another way: alienated from the Creator (Col.1:21), for each individual not only is life's end inevitable, but everlasting damnation beyond it. The tragedy is exacerbated by mankind's complete inability to rescue itself from this appalling dilemma. Death was promised (Gen.2: 17); death was received.

When the 'first parents' were driven from Eden in the white heat of holy indignation, and separated from God the Creator, mankind went with them (1 Cor.15:22). Cherubim guarded the Garden and the 'tree of life' with a flaming sword, underlining the impossibility of returning, except on God's terms (Gen.3:23,24). The matchless perfection belonging to the triune God alone had come into contact with Satan, and also mankind which the devil now claimed as his own (Ephes.2:2; Col.1:13). Humankind refuses to believe it, the horror too awful to contemplate, but as Satan is God's enemy so also is each individual who has yet to be rescued (Ps.7:11). The consequences are too profound, too appalling, for a human being to fully grasp. He still believes, and is encouraged to do so by the vast majority of his contemporaries (Matt.7:15), that God has turned a 'blind eye' to his original warning (Gen.2:17). Surely God still loves him, that he can crawl back into the divine favour (John 10: 1), can catch the eye with a good work or two (Ephes.2:8), or will arrive at heaven's 'Eden' to be greeted with a warm smile (Matt. 25:41)?

But that individual soul is DEAD (Gen.2:7): within the sin principle (Ephes.2:1), to obeying the moral law (James 2:10), to loving God with every fibre of his being (Deut.6:5; Matt.22:37,38), to worshipping his Creator (John 4:24), to hearing the voice of Christ

(John 10:27; 14:6; 18:37), to understanding the truth revealed by God (1 Cor.2:10). In short, man is cursed (Matt.25:41) and an enemy of heaven, a rebel and under the anger of the Divine from the moment life first wriggles in the womb. Should he be taken to Judgment in that state (Luke 12:20), he will be estranged everlastingly from God, in hell (Ps.9:17).

Nor does the matter stop at that point. A curse lies not only upon mankind, but also upon the entire creation that 'groans' under the weight of the condemnation (Rom.8:22): the dust from which man was formed (Gen.2:7), the tare-filled ground containing his corpse (Gen.3:17,18), and the animal kingdom he reigns over (Gen.1:26; 2:19,20).

The picture is bleak. Yet, there is hope! Deep within eternal ages past, as Solomon was able to relate to Sheba, 'while as yet he had not made the earth, nor the fields, nor the highest part of the dust of the world' (Prov.8:26), the Being of the triune God conceived a plan. At the appointed time, he would establish a nation in the midst of a fallen world, whose beauty would be holiness (1 Peter 2:9), and this was where one suspects Sheba's lessons began; God's first visit to Abram, and the covenantal promise that a 'great nation' would arise, in fact more than one (Gen.12:2; 17:6).

But first how was the justly offended God to be appeased, his anger assuaged? Or, how was Satan's hold over sinners to be broken, his kingdom overcome (Col.1:13), and man's rescue to be accomplished? The divine displeasure is not turned away with a wink, but demands satisfaction. At the same time, the Evil One would never relinquish power without a struggle of enormous proportions, and could the principle of sin be removed without the most profound of operations being performed? Thus, redemption's battlefield is covered in blood and strewn with the fallen.

In the light of this, it does not take intelligence long to realise that everything about the tabernacle – and the temple – can only be understood in terms of symbol; not least, the dissecting of the animal corpses. Aaron and his sons had laid their hands upon the bullock and the rams (Lev.8:14,18,22), and thus were identifying themselves with these animals that were about to be killed on their behalf, just as a ram had been substituted for Isaac (Gen.22:13).

The animals were being sacrificed that the sins of the men could be dealt with in the sight of heaven, not flicked from the carcase with a hand as one would a fleck of sand. To God sin is the heaviest and thickest commodity existing, therefore the sharpest of knives was used not only to slit the throat, but to penetrate the still warm flesh deeply and expertly cutting and slicing to the bone, the fatty tissue and the inwards separated from each other (Lev.8:14-25).

As sin permeated every recess of Aaron and his sons, so the knife did not spare anything within the animal carcases; as sin affected each part of their being ('heart...soul...might', Deut.6:5), so blood flowed freely from the beasts offered on their behalf. The 'fingers' of the flames carried the offerings heavenward, and the atoning blood poured out at the base of the altar offset the curse under which the ground lay (Gen.3:17).

Now the main part of the inauguration of the priesthood having been completed, Aaron and his sons were brought to the spotlight of personal commitment. As already noted, Moses daubed each man's tip of the right ear, the right thumb, and the big toe of the right foot (Lev.8:23,24). In the sight of heaven and the entire nation of Israel, symbolised was the intention of this priestly family to HEAR the commands of God (1 Sam.9:15), to LABOUR in his service and to WALK in his ways. They were now bound to the tabernacle, as at a later date the priests were to the temple, and every aspect of the religious life of the nation. Tragically, shortly afterwards two of the sons failed in this high calling (Lev.10:1,2).

In relating the account, Solomon could not have stopped at that point, but would have eagerly referred to one of his father's psalms, in which he envisaged the dedication of another whose 'ears' were opened to God's commands. This Person would also HEAR the voice from heaven (Ps.2:7; John 6:38), be ACTIVE in service (Ps.16:10; John 17:4), and TREAD the pathway paved for him (Ps.22:1-18; Matt.26:39). This great messianic truth had been revealed to David, passed on to Solomon - and in 'communing' with her host (1 Kings 10:2) would such remarkable news have been kept from Sheba? But, she might have asked, what had bread, cakes and a wafer to do with this solemn day (Exod.29:23-25)? Moses had produced a basket and from it had taken these items, and placed them upon the fat and right shoulder of the second ram, the ram of consecration. Then he placed this messy ingredient upon the hands of Aaron and his sons, who 'waved' them before the Lord, after which it ascended heavenward in flames (Lev.8: 26-28).

First, the priests had their sins dealt with, the bullock and the first ram shedding their blood and being offered on the altar of sacrifice on their behalf (Exod.29:10-14; Lev.8:14-21). Then, in the second ram, in whose blood strategic parts of their body were daubed, they were consecrated entirely to God and the place where he was to be worshipped (Exod.29:15-22; Lev.8:22-25). Now, parts of that ram were adorned with bread: the inner fat, signifying the depth of consecration, and the muscular right shoulder denoting the energy in the devotion (Exod.29:23-25; Lev.8:26-28).

As for the unleavened and oiled bread: bread, because this was the staple diet of the people (Gen.3:19), unleavened signifying purity (Ex.12:39; Matt.16:6; 1 Cor.5:6), and oil denoting God's special anointing (1 Sam.16:13). In other words, having had their sins 'covered' (all that could be hoped for in Old Testament times, Ps.32:1), and having been consecrated to God and to his 'house', the priests separated unto purity and consecration, were now dedicated to the service of the people. It all anticipated a High Priest of which Aaron was but a shadow (Heb.8:1-3), who would be of the purest (John 8:46), consecrated to his Father (John 8:29), and who would serve the people supremely (1 Tim.2:5; Heb.4:15; 5:2).

THE FIRE FOR SACRIFICE

Even if the detailed events of that day of consecration could not have been seen by the entire Hebrew nation (approximately over a million people present at the 'gate' of the tabernacle, Exod. 12:37), and a curtain barrier blocking the view, (Exod.27: 16), what occurred a few days later was seen by all the people without exception and brought them literally to their knees in awe and alarm (Lev.9).

They had become used to the unusual; had witnessed the miraculous on a grand scale whilst in Egypt (Exod.7-12), and entered the desert with the radiant cloud leading the way (Exod. 13:21); had seen the immovable Sinai shaken by the irresistible force of God's presence angelic hosts attending (Exod.19:16; Deut.33:1; Is.64:1-3), and now had watched the tabernacle erected in their midst (Exod.25-40:33). As a result, the nation had come to expect the unexpected, but perhaps what happened next was a dramatic surprise even to them.

A week had passed, and it was day one of the tabernacle's use, during which there had been a great deal of activity centred around the altar within the courtyard (the altar in the temple was thirty three feet square and ten feet high!). The nation had been summoned to appear once more at the 'gate', this time presenting appropriate animals for sacrifice (Lev.9:3-5), for no one in any age can expect other than heaven's retribution unless atonement has been made for them (John 8:24; Heb.9:22). At the same time, Aaron and his sons were realising how arduous was their calling as hours were spent slaughtering, and then sacrificing at the altar (Lev.9:8-21). Blood squelched beneath their feet (Lev.17:11), and sweat poured from their faces as they sweltered close to the flames of the altar and under the desert sun.

The day's events had ended with the new high priest, a hand raised, pronouncing a blessing upon the people (Lev.9:22), the benediction for which Aaron has always been noted: 'The Lord bless thee, and keep thee: The Lord make his face shine upon thee, and be gracious unto thee: The Lord lift up his countenance upon thee, and give thee peace. (Numb.6:23-26)' Then joined by Moses he entered the holy place of the tabernacle, for what purpose is not recorded, but probably in order to pray for what happened next (Luke 3:21,22). Something similar occurred when the temple was opened (2 Chron.5:13), as Solomon would have remembered.

Moses and Aaron reappeared in the sunlight and walked towards the crowds beyond the courtyard, who were doubtless silent with awe and watchful with excited curiosity. They saw Aaron's hand raised in blessing once again, and at that moment the site was bathed in the manifestation of God's presence (Lev.8:23); the pillar of cloud hovering over the scene radiating the beauty of holiness (Ps.29:2). There was no doubting what it was because its power was potent, the people incapable of standing (Exod.33:22; 34:5-8; 40:34,35), the experience witnessed in the temple (1 Kings 8:10,11).

At the same time, as the eye was dazzled by the display of purity and grace, a sound like a mighty wind assaulted the ear (Acts 2:1-3), as fire hurtled from heaven towards the courtyard (Lev.8:24). If not everyone in the nation had actually seen what had been taking place there that day, or the week before during the consecration of the priests, all were witnesses to the fact of the sacrifice's acceptance with God. They could not help but see what happened, as the flames' intensity erased what had been upon the altar (Lev.9:24).

Solomon understood what significance lay in the experience (as did a prophet after his day, 1 Kings 18:38), because he too had seen heaven pour out fire, and would he not have told Sheba about it? Like Moses and Aaron on that day when the tabernacle was inaugurated for the worship of God, he had also prayed when the temple's beauty was first publicly displayed (2 Chron.7:1). Both occasions were days of affirmation. Confirmed was the fact that God seeks and finds his elect (John 4:24), and that only through blood-sacrifice can they be accepted by him (Lev.17:11; Heb.9:22; 1 John 1:7). For 'hard questions' about the Lord's name to be answered correctly (1 Kings 10:1), Solomon must have taught Sheba these things. But what would Moses and Aaron have seen as they entered the tabernacle, and also what lay within the temple's 'holy place', and what did it signify? Sheba's curiosity would have wanted to be satisfied.

TEN

Tḥe Patḥway to tḥe Veil

But first, so much had been learned that when alone within the palace Sheba would have had opportunities to ponder the facts. The conclusion drawn from what she had heard was surely, 'what nation is there so great, who hath God so nigh unto them (Deut.4: 7)?' The Lord who had appeared remarkably to the patriarchs, to Moses and Aaron and the Israelites, as well as revealing truth to her host and his father had indeed 'loved Israel for ever' (1 Kings 10:9). To this 'holy nation' alone God had manifested himself as the one, true and only deity (Exod.20:3; Deut.6:4) especially favoured by his love (Deut.7:6-8), and granted custodianship of the truth he had revealed (Rom.3:1,2).

Likewise, to be assured of Jehovah's everlasting love for the Israelites (Jer.31:3; Mal.1:2), what great mysteries must Sheba have now understood: Abraham (Gen.12:1-3), Isaac and Jacob's (Gen.26:24; 28:13-15) relationship to the covenant of grace (Exod. 3:6); the natural depravity of mankind (Ps.14:1-3), and therefore the necessity of atonement (Lev.17:11); the significance of the priesthood and that of blood sacrifice (Exod.12:13; 28:41) – and the most mysterious, that there was a 'line' of salvation stretching from Adam through to Solomon and beyond their days (Gen.3:15; Ps.2:8) from which 'the seed' (Gen.3:15), the Messiah, would spring. And as for all this bloodletting and gore: she now realised the significance between this forthcoming 'seed', Abraham's 'only' son' and what occurred that day on Mount Moriah (Gen.22), and the activities that surrounded the altar of burnt offering (Lev.1-6).

THE WELL TRODDEN PATHWAY

Back in the desert, the flames from heaven having ignited the sacrificial offering upon the altar (Lev.9:24), throughout each day from the four quarters of the Israelite encampment a steady stream of people headed towards the curtained doorway of the tabernacle courtyard. They pulled what was probably an unwilling animal to be sacrificed as a BURNT offering, not that their sins might be erased, but as mentioned in the previous chapter, rather 'covered' until the next time (Ps.32:1). The concept of sin's eradication had yet to be fulfilled (1 John 1:7).

For those who could afford it the animal would have been a bullock or an ox (Lev.1), for most a lamb was sufficient, but the very poor carried doves or pigeons (Luke 2:22-24). These creatures though had not been chosen arbitrarily by their owners, but by God himself (Lev.1:2). Nor were the animals picked at random, but they had been especially examined before being removed from the pen or cage. For the burnt offering, they had to be male yearlings and without any physical blemish (Exod.12:5). From all that must have been explained to her, Sheba would now have known the reasons why.

Once at the curtained barrier of the tabernacle courtyard, the creature stood before its owner and one of the priests. It felt the owner's hand placed firmly upon its head, the sinner and the sacrificial victim closely identified with each other, and with this symbolic gesture the owner's confessed sin had been made over to it in the sight of God (Lev.1:3,4).

The animal was then taken into the courtyard, as the owner's appointed substitute, to be prepared for sacrifice as in the presence of God. The sharpness of the knife reminiscent of the one in Abraham's hand (Gen.22:10), drawn swiftly across the creature's throat, produced the necessary flow of warm blood which filled the bowl carried by the priest: a life poured forth, through a violent death (Gen.37:31-34), on behalf of the sinner (Lev.17:11). Solomon knew, and therefore Sheba surely did too, that his father had envisaged the Messiah suffering a violent death (Ps.22).

The priest then continued with the solemn proceedings. He took the bowl and liberally sprinkled the blood on all sides of the altar, as well as upon it, signifying the universal appeal of the sacrifice (Matt.20:16; 22:14; Acts 17:30). The wooden altar was about seven and a half feet square and four and a half feet high, and overlaid with brass. The wooden 'horns' on each corner, to which the sacrifice was tied (Ps.118:27), were also covered in brass as were the utensils used by the priests. A brass grate lay in the centre of the altar through which the remains of the sacrifice slithered.

With hundreds of such incidents taking place each day, the priests walked to and fro across a thick carpet of blood. But it had to be, because without the blood-shedding of the Victim there can be no remission of sins (Heb.9:22). The corpse was then flayed, before being expertly dissected (Lev.1:6). It was hard work, and sinners quickly realised the awfulness of sin, and therefore the extent of the atonement that had to be made in order to bring them back to God. Solomon was able to quote his father's graphic description of the Messiah's anguish: 'I am poured out like water, and all my bones are out of joint: my heart is like wax, it is melted in the midst of my bowels. My strength is dried up....and my tongue cleaveth to my jaws, and thou hast brought me into the dust of death' (Ps.22:14,15; Matt.27:34-50).

It also took time before the task was completed, and each part of the sacrifice was divided according to the law (Lev.1:12). The skin was ripped open and pulled free from the carcase, the head and legs severed from the body and the innards and fat cut from the bones. The sharp knife, with the deft movements of the expert, was plunged into the mass of flesh, cutting and slicing as it manoeuvred its way to the bone. How gruesome was the atoning sacrifice, but then, to what depths sin has reached!

The laver was only a few feet away (Exod.30:18), to which the priest carried the legs and the intestines for washing (Lev.1:9). A twofold symbolism was being observed. On the one hand, the fact that washing occurred before the flames consumed the victim on the altar, signified the purity of the Victim it was symbolising before he suffered and died (John 8:46). On the other, the close proximity of the altar to the laver signified the association of sanctification with justification (1 Cor.6:11); washing with regeneration (John 3:5; Titus 3:5).

The washing having been completed, the sacrifice was ready to be offered to God as 'a sweet savour' (Lev.1:9). By this time, so mangled was it the owner would not have recognized it as the animal he had brought to the priest (Is.52:14). It was a reminder of the havoc sin makes upon the soul.

Nothing could have illustrated the sufferings of the Messiah to Sheba, as foretold by David (Ps.22:1,2; Matt.27:46), more fully than the portrait of the priests busy at the altar in the blistering desert heat and close to the scorching ferocity of the flames that roared skywards. Each part of the offering was laid (with Abraham's meticulous care, Gen.22:9) in an orderly fashion on the wood already engulfed in fire (Lev.1: 7,8): the head, the fat, intestines, and the legs. The Messiah was not to be spared (Rom.8:32), the head and the fat symbolizing the external and internal aspects of his being, and the intestines and legs the inner and outer purity of his nature (John 8:46).

The priest carefully placed the mangled flesh and bone among the flames. There was nothing haphazard, or careless, about his action, because he understood that God demanded the sacrificial victim should be at the centre of the fire and at the hottest part of the conflagration, over the brass grating though which the ashes would fall. Only when the last of them had disappeared could it be said the action had been completed: 'finished' (John 17:4; 19:30).

The flesh saturated in blood and water at first sizzled its 'discomfort' (John 19:34), but soon the flames licked the offering dry of moisture (Ps.22:14,15; John 19:28) before surrendering to the inevitability of the fiery embrace. Soon, the blackened, charred embers dissolved into an unrecognisable heap that gradually edged its way through the grating and vanished from sight. The head of the offering the sinner had leaned upon not long before (Lev.1:4), which had borne his sin and guilt, had disappeared from sight and would never be seen again. The atonement was completed; it was 'finished' (John 19:30), and time for rejoicing (Numb.10:10).

Throughout each day of the forty years spent in the desert, the people saw smoke rising from the flaming 'fingertips' in the courtyard, curling upwards towards the cloudless sky, and knew that it reached deeply into the nostrils of God. The odour of burning flesh hung like a cloud over the entire encampment every hour of day and night, an unmistakeable smell that would have been intolerable had not the reasons for it been appreciated. The continual scent, a 'sweet savour unto the Lord' (Lev.1:9), was a constant reminder that he was delighted with his people. A covenant people, grounded in blood-sacrifice, must of necessity be a 'special people unto himself, above all people that are upon the face of the earth' (Deut.7:6).

The courtyard of either the tabernacle or the temple, so close to the sacred spot where the ark of the covenant stood in silent testimony to the holiness of God, was no place where the ordinary Israelite would desire to linger (Numb.17:13), even if permitted to do so. He was aware of the significance of the occasion: the solemn priests, the flaming heat, and the hiss of burning flesh. The sinner deserved the condemnation it all symbolized, but the victim had borne the brunt in his stead.

When the Hebrew arrived back at his tent, his wife was already preparing his next visit. It was the MEAT (meal) offering, which always accompanied that which had been burned, or followed soon after. The same procedure took place in Jerusalem's temple. The meat offering symbolized the grateful dedication of the sinner to God, his entire life and all his possessions, as a result of his sin having been 'covered' (Ps.32:1). For this reason the meat offering could never precede the other, for it is impossible for the unrepentant to commit their lives to God, as Cain discovered to his cost (Gen.4:3,5).

The meat offering always consisted of three ingredients, the main one being fine flour which had been shaken vigorously in the sieve, and the other two were oil and frankincense (Lev.2:1). As the individual made his way for the second time to the tabernacle, or at a later date the temple, he carried with him a highly valued treasure in God's sight. What finer 'flour' could there be than a life strenuously sifted by the hand of God, and placed under the microscope of the moral, ceremonial and judicial laws – and found to be sinless? Sheba would have been reminded of David's Psalm, in which he 'hears' the Messiah 'delighting' to do the will of God (John 8:29), and testifying, 'thy law is within my heart' (Ps.40:8).

As Aaron and his sons had been anointed with oil (Lev.8: 12,30; Ps.133:2), so too was the flour for the meat offering. It signified the anointing of God the Spirit (1 Sam.16:13) and separation to God in his service that results from it (Matt.3:13-17); and is not the Messiah considered to be anointed by God 'with the oil of gladness' above his fellows (Ps.45:7; Heb.1:9)? Then sprinkled upon the flour was the precious gift of frankincense, symbolizing adoration and deity (Matt.2:11), something which Sheba with the 'incense road' in mind would have appreciated.

But there were three companions, not just two, and they followed in that order and were never divided: the burnt, the meat, and the peace offerings (Lev.3). Sins having first been 'covered', and the sinner and his possessions then being dedicated to the One who covered them (Rom.12:1), now in the PEACE offering understandable and joyful thanksgiving was expected.

Two other offerings followed in their wake, both of them a constant reminder of the penetrating nature of true holiness. This too Sheba learned, because Solomon would have taught her that 'the eyes of the Lord are in every place, beholding the evil and the good' (Prov.15:3). In EVERY place, and ALL of the time (Ps.33: 13)? Such an idea would have been a strange one to his guest, and to all of Israel's neighbours as well, for although idols possess eyes nothing can they see at any time (Ps.115:5)!

Until her visit to Jerusalem she would not have been aware of the concept of omniscience and omnipresence, but now Solomon would surely have outlined to her the unique revelation given to his father David; that nowhere was it possible to escape the divine gaze of perfect righteousness, even if one was to 'take the wings of the morning, and dwell in the uttermost parts of the sea.' God knows where one is, and what one is doing, each second of every day: nothing alludes him, and he never slumbers nor sleeps (Pss.121:3; 139:1-14). That was an astonishing thought at the time.

The SIN offering served to underline that truth. The deceitfulness of sin is such, and the sinner so affected by it, much sinfulness is unrecognised (John 9:41). However, God knows about it, and condemns each heart as 'desperately wicked' (Jer.17:9,10). Perhaps though the individual is ignorant of the offence, or unaware of the motive's impurity. The sin offering then was brought to the priest in recognition of the subtle nature of the sin principle (Lev.4; 1 John 1:9).

The searching though continued (does it ever cease?). How many failings in the sinner's life are glossed over and not considered sins at all, secreted away and known only to the individual, the one offended, and to the Quiet Observer (1 Sam.16: 7)? To take several examples: the abusing of one's neighbour behind the scenes, privately deceiving him (1 Kings 21), the covert misuse of his property (2 Kings 6:5), and the breaking of promises to him (Prov.20:7). The TRESPASS offering, together with appropriate remuneration, catered for these misdemeanours (Lev.6: 1-7).

(Once the Israelites entered the promised land another offering was introduced, the DRINK offering (Numb.15:1-7), which was 'strong wine poured unto the Lord' (Numb.28:7). This ceremony was separate from the others, although never performed in isolation, but was an addition. Its purpose was to 'cheer God and man' (Judg.9:13), that is, when poured over the sacrifice everyone involved was concurring in the greatness of atonement (1 Sam.10: 3), and the joyfulness its fruitfulness produces John 15:11.)

In the light of these offerings having to be presented for sacrifice, the sinner made his way to the tent of the congregation, and later the temple, realising how distant he was by nature to the heart of God (Is.1:13), how insensitive to his presence (Ephes.2:1). Yet, at the same time, how gracious is Jehovah (Exod.33:19) to provide the means for ALL sin to be covered (1 John 1:7), nothing left to be condemned (Rom.8:1) when as Solomon would have reminded

Sheba 'every secret thing, whether it be good, or whether it be evil' shall be brought to judgment (Eccles.12:14).

WITHIN THE SANCTUARY

In contrast to the constant activity within the courtyard - the intensity of concentrated effort must have been tangible - a quiet stillness prevailed inside the holy place. Outside were sweating priests, nervous animals, killing, dissecting, heaving and humping, as well as the stench of burning flesh, sizzling blood and billowing smoke – but only a few paces away was an area of mystery and tranquillity.

There were good reasons why the holy place maintained its aura of mystery. The first was that only the priests were permitted to enter it. In any case, the wall of the courtyard restrained idle curiosity, and even its entrance had across it a curtained barrier. How often from afar (Josh.3:3,4), when the tabernacle moved on (Exod.40:36), the people had glimpsed the Levites going about their sacred business in dismantling and at the next encampment assembling it, but the lingering look was never encouraged (Numb. 3:4; 17:13)

But then, nobody could prevent the thought processes from being occasionally curious. After all, everyone was aware it was a place of 'power and glory' (Ps.63:2). As those responsible for making the tabernacle furniture had been chosen by God from among the ordinary people (Exod.36:2), it must be assumed that what was inside the holy place was common knowledge, but not being able to look inside this restricted area must have stimulated speculation.

It contained just three major articles – the seven-branched candlestick, the table of shewbread, and the altar of incense (Exod. 37:10-29) – but what was their function, and more important, what mysterious significance did they possess? Again, what did the priests DO once inside this 'sanctuary' (Heb.9:2)? Whatever it was there was an element of danger attached to it, and the sight of two dead priests being carried out underlined that notion (Lev.10:1-5).

To begin with, following the example set by Moses when at the burning bush (Exod.3:5), the priests were always barefooted when ministering (very needful in the courtyard where they continually walked on blood; in itself of great significance), but particularly so when entering the sanctuary.

Once inside, the first thing they would have noticed was the absence of windows, the rays of the sun having no place here. But to offset the absence of nature's light, seven flames flickered from sockets on an ornate candlestick situated on the sanctuary's south side. It was the only source of light in that small area.

LIGHT IN THE DARKNESS

The candlestick was a single piece of beautifully constructed craftsmanship. It was about five feet tall and three and a half feet wide, and consisted of a main shaft or stem from which six 'branches' protruded at three different levels, three on each side of the stem. Sockets were situated at the top of the stem, and at the end of each 'branch': seven in all. Every Israelite knew the number signified completion (Gen.1:31; Numb.8:1-4).

These 'seven lamps of fire' revealed a glorious piece of work (Rev.4:5), and of vastly superior quality to the 'molten calf' made by the Israelites during a dark period (Exod.32:4). Of gold beaten into shape (Exod.31:1-4), it was richly adorned with raised work of golden knobs, flowers and little bowls resembling half an almond shell. To accompany the candlestick were golden tongs for the removal of the charred ends of the wicks, and golden dishes in which to place these 'snuffings', as well as golden vessels to contain the pure olive oil required for the lighting of the lamps (Exod.25:31-40).

The reason for lighting them though was not merely practical, supplying light within a darkened area, but from the start God revealed there was a spiritual dimension behind the presence and use of the seven-branched candlestick. The priests were aware of it. They knew they were participating in no less than an everlasting statute on behalf of the children of Israel (Exod.27:21), and therefore understood why the rays of the sun were kept at bay; the light of nature not permitted to compete with the light of grace.

It was no doubt to emphasise this fact that within the holy place of the temple in Jerusalem there was not one candlestick of pure gold, but ten, each of identical design to that situated in the tabernacle (1 Kings 7:49). It was a humble foretaste of the glory to be experienced within the HEAVENLY Jerusalem (Rev.21:23).

The priest entered the sanctuary each morning, probably before the encampment had stirred, as well as at the end of the day. When he did so, upon approaching the candlestick with the vessel containing pure oil in his hand he understood the threefold symbol behind his action. Likewise, the priest who entered the sanctuary in the temple understood too. 'LET THERE BE LIGHT!' was the first command creation heard, 'and there WAS light' (Gen.1:3).

To begin with, many through the ages have mistakenly assumed that LOVE is the attribute most associated with God, but in fact LIGHT is the most noticeable 'garment' he wears (Ps.104:2; 1 John 1:5), and light so glorious and penetrating sinners quickly discover it is 'unapproachable' (1 Tim.6:16).

To provide a few examples: it was 'glory' that first appeared to Abraham, not love (Acts 7:2; 9:3). Likewise, although his grandson Jacob had been visited by the Lord in a dream and believed the spot where he stood was 'the gate of heaven', his audible response was not about divine love, but rather 'How dreadful is this place! (Gen.28:17)'.

Again, Moses' first experience of God was through flaming light, not assurances of love (Exod.3: 1-6), and on another occasion after being in God's presence so radiant was his face he was obliged to wear a veil when speaking to the people. They were fearful of looking at Moses, not because he radiated love, that they could have borne, but on the contrary, what they glimpsed was blinding light (Exod.34:29-35; Acts 22:6). Or, what of Samson's mother? Upon seeing the second Person of the Trinity in the form of the angel of the Lord she told her husband her Visitor's face was like that of an angel of God. In other words, she saw the radiance of light, but did it express love, and was she therefore comforted? She testified that the sight was 'very terrible' (Judg.13:6).

The divine light then, 'very terrible', and 'dreadful', sheds rays of holiness with the intensity of white heat (1 Cor.3:13), exposing the slimmest of shadows and intolerant of them (1 John 1:5). It is as likely to be approachable as the priest's hand would have been to linger in the seven flames of the candlestick. Flame licking flesh is but a small yet painful reminder of what an unredeemed soul experiences eternally when touched by the light of Ultimate Purity. Then again the priest would have had something else in mind; not only thoughts about holiness, but marvelling at the fact he had some understanding of the nature of God; of what constitutes that special quality. He could not have fathomed the information for himself, or trusted others to discover it for him; he could only have groped in circles within the darkness of his natural ignorance. Such insights are the prerogative of heaven to reveal (1 Cor.2:12), and what if this had not been accomplished? No other nation upon earth could testify, as the Israelites had done through Moses, that they had actually heard the voice of almighty God: 'out of the midst of the fire' (Deut.5:24-26); that is, the flaming bush and the fiery mount (Exod.3:2-4; 19:18). Those seven small flames that flickered in the holy place, then, symbolised perfect righteousness revealing absolute truth, and nothing can blaze whiter than Truth: the communication of the mind and heart of God, his thoughts and feelings (1 Cor.3:13). Nor is anything more capable of reaching deeper profundity than that which issues from God's 'mouth' (Deut.8:3), as One greater than Moses (Heb.3:3) was later to declare (Matt.4:4). And were his disciples not baptized with fire (Matt.3:11; Acts 2:3)?

FOOD ON THE TABLE

Across the way from the golden candlestick stood a table, three feet long, eighteen inches wide, and two and a quarter feet tall, its importance underlined by the fact that in his writings Moses mentions it twenty-one times referring to it as 'pure' (Lev.24:6). Attached to it were two staves of acacia wood overlaid with gold, which rested in golden rings (Exod.25:23,26, 27).

Like so much else in the tabernacle and the temple, the table was also made of gold-covered acacia wood (1 Kings 7:48): in fact, of 'pure gold' (Exod.25:24). Around its edge were two borders, of the same precious material ('a crown of gold'), one on top of the other. If one was decorative, the lower of the two was for a practical purpose, to prevent items on the table from sliding off.

What lay there was unleavened bread, twelve loaves, which God commanded were to be continually set before him (Exod.25:30). Hence, it was known as 'showbread', 'the bread of setting before'. The loaves, made of the finest of flour and either oblong or square-shaped, were placed in two piles or in two rows, six loaves apiece. Incense in a golden bowl adorned each pile or row.

The bread remained upon the table undisturbed until the Sabbath, when a priest replaced it with fresh loaves, but not one crumb was discarded. The loaves had been offered to God, and were therefore eaten in his presence by the sanctified priests (Lev. 24:8,9), reflecting the privileged fellowship they enjoyed with him (Lev.10:12,13).

As each day the priests passed between the candlestick and the table, and were aware of the significance of the former, they must also have understood aspects of that which was associated with the latter: the covering of gold, golden bowls containing incense, golden rings supporting gold-covered staves, and what of the loaves, and the fact they were eaten by the priests? Were these not questions which required answering to an enquiring Sheba? Gold, incense, bread: what significance could they possibly have in common?

Everywhere Sheba looked during her visit to Jerusalem, and many areas where even she would not have been permitted to enter, gold glistened. Within the temple and the palaces, adorning the royal family and the courtiers: everywhere. But this was no surprise. In fact, as a visitor to Solomon's court Sheba had added to the glister; a generous gift of twenty talents (1 Kings 10:10). It was expected, an expression of friendliness between two countries. So when told the table of 'shewbread' was adorned with gold, as were the bowls resting upon the loaves of bread, the staves and the rings they rested in as well as the dishes, spoons and covers (Exod.25: 29), Sheba would not have been surprised.

However, the more subtle references might have stimulated an enquiring mind. For example, why was bread placed on the table, and why did the loaves always number twelve? Why was the table referred to as 'pure' (Lev.24:6)? In any case, why place bowls of incense upon the bread? Clearly, as with the altar, laver, and candlestick, mysterious significance surrounded the small table. Sheba already understood that gold was associated with royalty, and coming from 'the land of spices' she would have known incense was associated with deity (Matt.2:11). As for the bread, everyone knew this was the staff of life (Gen.3:19); incense placed upon it signified the life of God. These loaves then symbolised 'the true bread from heaven', that which nourishes at the deepest level (John 6:32,35).

For that reason Sheba could easily have understood the symbolism behind the regular replenishing of the bread, why it was made of FINE flour and placed upon a 'PURE' table (Lev.24: 5,6), and why the priests ate the loaves. They, whose calling it was to intercede for the people, stood each week in the presence of God to eat 'the true bread' which in turn interceded for THEM. Thus, during those moments, the nation's unity in Jehovah was being signified, and the 'new Israel' presciently anticipated: the 'Israel of God' (Gal.6: 16), the 'royal priesthood', the 'holy nation' (1 Peter 2:9) and the 'kingdom of priests' (Rev 1:6): in short, the Christian Church.

But the table had still not completed its story. The messianic hope of which Israel was the custodian (Rom.3:1) was known to both David and Solomon, and through her 'communing' had now been passed on to Sheba (1 Kings 10:1-3); that the Messiah would suffer and die on the 'altar' of sacrifice (Ps.22), and then arise and ascend (Pss.16:10,11; 110:1) back to the Father (Ps.2:7; Heb.5:5) who had eternally delighted in him (Prov.8:30). But now her thoughts, and heart, were gradually being led towards the most profound of all intimacies: the knowledge of God.

She had first been introduced to the altar and laver, where she had been taught about the Messiah's work, but then from the courtyard she had 'entered' the holy place to confront not only his work but his person. First, a pen-portraiture: the candlestick with its SEVEN flames shedding the light of perfect holiness and absolute truth (John 1: 14). The world would never have experienced anything like it, heaven's favoured Son (Matt.3:17) standing amidst men as a man (Heb.4:15), yet sinless (John 8:46)! The PROPHET, Faithful and True (Rev.19:11), would proclaim his Father's Word (John 7:16); that truth he had heard from within the Godhead (John 18:37).

Then the larger frame: the Messiah as PRIEST, in fact a most extraordinary one, whose character was signified in the 'purity' of the table (Lev.24:5,6) upon which lay the generous provision of bread 'uncorrupted' by leaven (Matt.16:6-12). However, the uniqueness of this Anointed One lay not solely in his moral perfection, but particularly in that he would be the possessor of two natures, the divine and the human. Hence, the golden bowls containing incense resting upon the basic requirement each human needs to sustain life (Prov.28:19). Had the bowls been opened, or broken (Matt.26:7), the 'scent' of deity would have permeated each crumb of the loaves beneath them (Mark 14:3), as well as every nook and cranny of the house of worship (Is.6:1-4). Little wonder then the table was bordered by 'a crown of gold' (Exod.25:24), indeed 'many crowns' (Rev.19:12), while the incense containers occupied the central position on the table. And they were placed ABOVE the bread, not beneath it, theological correctness demanding the elevation of the one symbol over the other.

Yet the two were inexorably linked, the golden bowls resting upon the loaves (Lev.24:7), and not placed elsewhere on the table. The Messiah would represent God before man, and man in the presence of God (Heb.4:14-16; 12:2): God the Son (Mark 2:1-7) and the Son of man (Luke 19:10), divine and human (Exod.3:14; John 8: 58), in harmony the one with the other. To divide the two natures was to have registered the messianic hope hope-less (John 1:1-14).

The Messiah would make his appearance on the world's stage not this time as the Angel of God (Exod.14:19), but in flesh and blood (Luke 24:39). Yet he would arrive like the manna from heaven which nourished the Israelites each day, and just as unobtrusively (Exodus 16:14,15; John 8:32), without the least taint of natural 'leaven' (Matt.16:6; John 8:46), the whitest 'flour' of his character having been shaken unscathed in the 'sieve' of daily temptations (Heb.4:15).

He was to be the 'true bread' (John 6:32), ordained to be wrenched into pieces for the salvation of sinners (Matt.26:26), the matter settled in heaven before time began; David having revealed to him that the Son would delight to do the will of the Father (Ps. 40:8; John 6:38). But the twelve loaves upon the 'pure table' (Lev. 24:6), one per tribe, were not mere exhibits in a museum. They were a symbol of the most vital experience known to man: knowing God, intimately (John 14:17,20) and eternally (John 17:3).

The 'hungry' beneficiaries therefore would receive this greatest of gifts as participants, not leaving 'the bread' upon 'the table', but eating it and relishing every morsel. In this way, the 'Bread' and the beneficiaries become one (Ephes.5:30), as his saving ministry would be made over to them (John 15:5). They would never 'hunger' again (John 6:33-35). In other words, when the priests ate the loaves each week in the presence of God (Lev.24:9), on their own behalf and that of the people (and the bread could not get closer to the priests than that!), they were symbolising an astonishing truth.

Sheba, in her quest, was being informed this act of the priests revealed God intended that eventually each one of his people would be drawn into the closest proximity to him; not the greatest and most important of them only, but the weakest and the youngest too (Ezek.36:25-27). No longer would the people of God be restrained by barriers (Exod.19:12), watching from afar (Heb.12:20), but instead their motto would be 'Know the Lord! (Jer.31:34)' In fact, 'knowing' him so intimately that the Messiah would one day say, 'At that day (the descent of God the Spirit, Acts 2), ye shall know that I am IN my Father, and ye IN me, and I IN you (John 14:20).' It is indeed a 'mystical union'.

AT THE VEIL

There was a third item of furniture within the holy place, situated as close to the veil as possible; that ornately decorated partition shielding the sacred area from view (Exod.26:33; 30:6). It was another altar, 'most holy', standing three feet tall, a foot and a half in length and breadth, and overlaid with pure gold (Exod.30:3, 10).

It was the altar of incense. Like the other altar outside in the courtyard, at each corner were 'horns', and like the table of shewbread it too possessed wooden staves sheathed in gold which rested in two golden rings on either side, while its surface was also bordered by 'a crown of gold'. On the altar was a golden vessel containing crushed 'sweet incense', which smouldered all day and throughout the night because of the embers it rested upon, brought by the priest first thing each morning from the other altar; the daily procedure unchanged with the building of the temple, it was a 'perpetual incense' (Exod.30:8).

But why were there two altars, and was there significance in the fact that one was outside and the other indoors? The answers are not difficult to discover. God's dealings with his people, from Adam (Gen.3:21) to Aaron (Lev.16), reveal the impossibility of seeking to approach him without first atonement having been made (1 Tim.6:16; Heb.9:22). Thus, one could not have entered the holy place in the tabernacle or the temple without first passing the altar of burnt offering. Salvation always precedes sanctification.

Once the altar had been passed, the finger flames pointing the sacrificial offering to heaven, then and only then was it possible for the priests to enter the holy place and be introduced to the symbolism pertaining to the messianic hope: the seven-branched candlestick ('O send out thy light and thy truth', Ps.43: 3; John 1:1-14), the table of shewbread ('The meek shall eat and be satisfied ...' Ps.22:26; John 6:35). And what of the third item of furniture? For the high priest and his colleagues, serving in such a sanctified environment, it was reflected in the yearning of the psalmist and every child of God since: 'How amiable are thy tabernacles, O Lord of hosts! My soul longeth, yea, even fainteth for the courts of the Lord, my heart and my flesh crieth out for the living God...thine ALTARS, O Lord of hosts, my King, and my God. Blessed are they that dwell in thy house, they will be still praising thee. (Ps.84:1-4)'

Emanating from the altar outside was the repellent odour of burning flesh and blood, the stench of sin being dealt with, but from the altar within the sanctuary arose the scent of worship and praise, of sin having been dealt with. Familiar to Solomon, and now to Sheba, was the exultant cry of thanksgiving: 'Then will I go unto the ALTAR of God, unto God my exceeding joy; yea, upon the harp will I praise thee, O God my God. (Ps.43:4)'

The sweetness of the scent permeated the entire sanctuary, arising from the golden censer (Rev.8:3), indicating the breadth of God's presence, the depth of the worship and the extent of the thanksgiving the 'royal priesthood' is in a position to give (1 Peter 2:9,10). In the words of Solomon's father: 'Let my prayer be set forth before thee as incense, and the lifting up of my hands, as the evening sacrifice' (Ps.141:2).

But there was something else of singular significance. The small altar was a short distance from the veil, its location by no means arbitrarily selected. In fact, it stood like a sentinel outside the MOST holy place, and close to the entrance. Thus the high priest was incapable of gaining an entrance into the 'Holiest of all' (Heb.9:3), where stood the sacred ark of the covenant (Exod.25:10 -22), without first acquainting himself with the altar a few feet away on the other side of the veil.

The reason for this was clarified, as with the 'shewbread' table, in the understanding of the symbolism. Three important facets of this item of the sanctuary's furniture were prominent: the appearance of gold, the presence of the incense, and of its 'sweetness' wafting vertically. In short, kingship and deity ascending to God (Matt.2:11; John 18:36,37; Acts 1:9).

But how is that possible, deity ascending to deity, Sheba might have asked? Then the mysterious revelation given to David, undoubtedly taught her by Solomon, would have sprung to mind: 'THE LORD saith unto MY LORD, Sit thou at my right hand, until I make thine enemies thy footstool' (Ps.110:1). 'The Lord', 'my Lord', and was her quest not about 'the name of THE LORD' (1 Kings 10:1)?

And who was David's 'Lord'? The tabernacle, and the temple Sheba was admiring, revealed who it was. The Son (Ps.2:7) in agony under a blackened sky crying to the Father (Ps.22:1; Luke 23:44); the Victim whose sacrificial merit would reach heaven in the 'flames' of suffering and death (Ps.22:13-18; 2 Cor.5:21); the Victor over the tomb itself, whose corpse would be incorruptible (Ps.16:10; 1 Cor.15:54); the triumphant One rising again and ascending in the 'sweetness' of his purity, to discover 'fullness of joy' and 'pleasures for evermore' at 'the right hand' of Israel's God (Ps.16:11; Heb.12:2).

No more authoritative position could he possess, and what would he be doing at the 'right hand' of the everlasting throne (Rev.4:2)? The candlestick had already revealed, that as the Messiah he would be the Prophet bearing witness to truth (John 18:37), the table that he would be the Priest interceding on behalf of his people (Zech.3:1-

4), and now the altar upon which rested the frankincense testified he was the King. In fact the King-Priest (Zech.6:13), King over all kings (Rev.19:16) and Priest over all priests (Exod.28), the divine and eternal High Priest (Ps,110:1). In which case, his intercession at the throne on behalf of his elect people would be everlasting (Heb.4:15).

But what mysteries lay beyond the veil?

ELEVEN
Where Two Realms Meet

'You're nearer to God in a garden than anywhere else on earth.'
The equivalent of that sentiment was more than likely known
to Sheba and her people back in Marib, the pagan world
understandably assuming that the pathway through creation's beauty
leads eventually to Deity.

On the surface nothing could be more evident, and thus the
worship of the pagan gods always entails the adoration of nature.
Myriads of sparkling galaxies (Ps.147:4), the yellow sun and silvery
moon (Ps.8:3) hanging in black spaciousness as if by threads;
countless birds swooping in blue skies, and numerous green and
brown landscapes vibrant with creatures great and small. How vast
an area nature inhabits, and how many the gods to be discovered
there! Sheba herself had spent her entire life gazing adoringly up at
the cream-coloured Ilumquh!

It was therefore a tremendous cultural shock (one of many she
had experienced since her arrival in Jerusalem) to learn not only of
her god's irrelevance, but that Jehovah alone is Lord (Deut. 6:4;
Ps.135:5) who considered Ilumquh an enemy (Exod.20:3; Is. 42:8).

As if that was not sufficient to shake her, Sheba also learned that although nature illustrates the Creator's existence (Job 38:4; Rom. 1:20) it is incapable of introducing him even to the sincere seeker. Thunders rolling, lightning flashing, earth quaking, winds whistling and man trembling: none of these, in themselves, are capable of bringing him closer to the Creator. None.

Like most people confronted with this dilemma, Sheba could have asked, 'How is it possible, then, to know him (Matt.19:25)?', and God himself supplied the answer to Moses: 'I will be gracious to whom I will be gracious, and will shew mercy on whom I will shew mercy. (Exod.33:19)' Sheba had already learned from Solomon of his father's maxim, that it is God's prerogative to make himself known: 'Salvation belongeth unto the Lord… (Ps.3: 8; Rom.9:17)'. In fact, he leaves the majority to seek 'comfort' from their gods, as is their desire (Matt.20:16).

For example, moments before Abraham received his sudden and unexpected visitation (Gen.12:1; Acts 7:2), his household figurines were his chief delight (Josh.24:2). Likewise, at the time when Moses inquisitively approached the burning bush (Exod.3:1-3), Egyptian culture governed his thinking (Acts 7:22). Neither Abraham or Moses – and the many others who had similar experiences, John 6:45,65 - sought the true God. In fact they were unaware of his existence, until that moment he appeared before them. Then they discovered, no doubt to their astonishment, they had featured in his eternal plan even before time began (John 1:48, 49; 1 John 4:10).

The same principle applied to the mighty nation of Israel, one that the people were reminded of during the wilderness wanderings (Deut.7:6-8), that its existence was entirely due to the grace of God. This 'holy people' (1 Peter 2:9) had nothing about which to boast, least of all numerical greatness, because compared to the other nations Israel was small. Rather, Jehovah's everlasting love for this 'special people' (Jer.31:3) was the sole reason why they were recipients of his mercy.

As a result the widest of chasms, a 'great gulf fixed' (Luke 16:26), existed between the treasured elect and the benighted heathen (Mal.3:17,18). The Israelites worshipped the Creator who had 'found' them (Gen.12:1-3; John 4:24), their enemies 'served the creature' whom they had discovered (Rom.1:25); the 'peculiar people' walked in the 'marvellous light' of revealed truth (Ps.119: 105; 1 Peter 2:9; 3 John 4), the outsiders groped in the intense darkness of ignorance (John 3:19).

But most significant of all: whereas nature's ubiquitous 'deities' dwelt in vast open spaces, leaving the adherents to hunt for them - the expansive firmament (2 Kings 21:3,4), the fearsome elements (Lev.18:21; 2 Kings 21:6), the cluster of trees (Jer.10:1-3) or the mountain ranges (1 Kings 11:7; 18:20-28) – Jehovah did the entirely unexpected. He always does (Is.55:8). He localised his presence, beckoning to his people to join him, leaving them in no doubt as to the location of the venue.

From their captivity in Egypt they followed Moses to a particular spot, Sinai (Exod.19), and now in the wilderness he gave assurance that he would meet them again, not from a distance upon the heights of a mountain, but from within a very limited space. True, the glory that was uniquely his forbad spiritual intimacy, and demanded an intercessory agency, but nevertheless the people were pointed to an actual place where their Lord could be found. In fact, as Solomon and Sheba 'communed' with each other in close proximity (1 Kings 10:2), so too did God promise to 'commune' with his chosen nation (Exod.25:22). That venue, both in the temple as well as in the tabernacle, was known for obvious reasons as 'the MOST holy place' (Exod.26:33; Heb.9:3).

OPENING THE VEIL

The thoughts of the high priest that moment he gently pulled aside the heavy veil, just wide enough for him to gain entrance to this most sacred area, can only be imagined. Of all the people he alone was permitted to enter. The fact that he did so annually on the tenth day of the seventh month (Lev.23:27,28), on the great Day of Atonement (Lev.16), the most important event in the Israelite calendar, served to underline the gravity of what he was doing. Reverential awe coupled to fearful apprehension: these emotions probably best described how he felt.

However before he arrived at the veil, as has been noted with 'HOLINESS TO THE LORD' written upon his headgear as well as upon his heart (Exod.28:36), he had already visited three vitally important places; first the laver. He washed thoroughly, and then removing his priestly garments, clothed himself in white linen. Next he visited the altar standing nearby, where atonement was made for the people as well as for himself (Lev.16:11).

He then poured the blood from the sacrifice into a bowl set aside for the purpose (Heb.9:7), and carrying it, passing the seven flames of the candlestick and the twelve loaves on the table, he made his way to the other altar, and there from the bowl in his hand he daubed the 'horns' protruding from each corner with the blood. Smouldering 'coals' had also been brought from the altar of burnt offering, and when the incense was applied to these a mist of sweet scent billowed from the golden censer (Lev.16:12). Thus, having visited the altar close to the veil, with its symbolism of blood-sacrifice and priestly intercession (Exod.30:10) coupled to thankfulness and praise (Ps.141:2), the high priest was ready to enter the most mysterious room in the world.

As he did so, only one sound could be heard within the sanctuary, and that came from the hem of his blue outer garment worn beneath the ephod; shoulder pieces woven with threads of beaten gold, fastened together, and reaching nearly to the knee, (Exod.28:6-8). Around the hem of that garment were pomegranates arranged alternately in colours of blue, purple and scarlet, and between each one was a very small golden bell, that tinkled with every swish of the garment. To those near enough to hear, it revealed his movements as he undertook his ministerial duties; not solely for their edification, but as a personal discipline, lest being unseen by his fellow men he should be tempted to loiter (Exod.28: 33-35). The tragedy involving Aaron's two sons must always have been uppermost in the family's memory, if not that of the entire nation (Lev.10:1-7).

BEYOND THE VEIL

God's anointed servant, whose regalia testified to an honoured ministry 'for glory and for beauty' (Exod.28:40), stepped over the threshold. What greeted him was solemn stillness, made more sombre when contrasted with the unceasing sounds a large encampment could not fail to make (Exod.12:37), even during religious observance. The animal kingdom in any case is no respecter of occasions. Then he would have been aware of the unusual shape of the room, but not surprised, because 'the most holy place' was designed by the Most Holy himself (Exod.25:9; Heb.9:23). And there must have been a reason, although not difficult to discover, why the area's measurements were those of a perfect cube: fifteen feet in length, and also in breadth: the 'Holiest of all', where God manifested his presence each year (Heb.9:3), reflecting Solomon's famous phrase, 'the heaven of heavens' where Jehovah dwells eternally (1 Kings 8:49; Rev.21:16).

Just a few paces away from where the high priest stood was Israel's most precious ornament, 'the ark of the covenant' (Exod. 25:10-22). It was a box made of acacia wood, and as one would expect overlaid with pure gold, and for such a grand and venerated object was small, just three feet and three quarters long, two feet and a quarter wide and two feet and a quarter tall. It was surmounted by a plate of solid gold, the renowned 'mercy seat' upon which God had promised to manifest himself (Exod.25:22), and surveying the scene on either end as angelic 'witnesses' were two golden cherubim (Deut.17:6), their wings spread over the 'mercy seat' (Exod.25:20). A border - or 'crown' - of gold also encircled the ark near the top (Exod.25:10,11), and like the table of shewbread had gold-covered wooden staves in golden rings attached to each side. These were removed when the temple was built, as a sign that the nation had at last arrived home, the travelling days over (1 Kings 8:8).

So intrinsically bound up with Israel's history was the ark, that to trace what happened to it is to measure the spiritual welfare of the nation. For example, how encouraged were the people in Jehovah at that early period, when they heard the order from Moses for the ark to be lifted and placed upon the shoulders of the Levites in readiness for moving on: 'Rise up Lord, and let thine enemies be scattered, and let them that hate thee flee before thee' (Numb.10: 35), a prayer close to David's own heart (Ps.68:1). And when the people saw it (albeit covered, and from 2000 cubits distance) how triumphant they felt, as when they entered Canaan (Josh.3:1-4), or upon arrival at the gates of Jerusalem under David's leadership: 'Arise, O Lord, into thy rest, thou and the ark of thy strength. Let thy priests be clothed with righteousness, and let thy saints shout for joy' (2 Sam.6:15,16; Ps.132:8,9).

The cry had ascended to the guards upon the bulwarks, 'Lift up your heads, O ye gates, and be ye lift up ye everlasting doors, and the King of glory shall come in.' But the 'password' was required: 'Who is this King of glory?' and the reply was heard, 'The Lord strong and mighty, the Lord mighty in battle. Lift up your heads, O ye gates, even lift them up, ye everlasting doors, and the King of glory shall come in.' The guards though were vigilant, enquiring a second time: 'Who is this King of glory?' they shouted back. Permission was granted to enter the city when the 'password' was provided once more, 'The Lord of hosts, he is the King of glory' (Ps.24:7-10).

By the sharpest of contrasts though, how tragic was the situation when the ark was captured, and by Israel's most dangerous enemy too. It had no business being in the front line of battle, but with the Philistines winning, the nation's declension was such even the leaders suggested using the sacred emblem as a talisman. From its resting place in the most holy place at Shiloh (Josh.18:1) it was taken to the battlefield, but instead of encouraging the Israelites, its presence stimulated the Philistines to fight harder! The ark was carried off, and 'Ichabod' ('The glory is departed from Israel') was written across the nation (1 Sam.4).

The ark was vital to an understanding of what Sheba sought, it would therefore have featured prominently in the discussions between herself and Solomon. Would she not have been taught something of its history, for an example, David's account of what happened to thousands of Israelites when their curiosity caused them to look inside the strange box? It had suddenly arrived back from Philistine territory after its capture, and the citizens of Bethshemesh were understandably excited by its return. Nevertheless, they paid a high price for their audacity. They were struck down in judgment (1 Sam.5 - 6).

And what of Uzzah? In seeking to steady the ark when on its journey from Gibeah to Jerusalem, he touched it. David watched the man drop dead (2 Sam.6:1-11). On the surface it appeared a harsh measure, but the lesson was being taught that the Realm above ought never to be trifled with by the realm below (John 8: 23).

LIFTING THE LID

The most holy place, whether in the tabernacle or the temple, was the epicentre of the nation's life, and each Israelite's mind (Matt.6:21). From first light to nightfall, however hectic the daily tasks uppermost in every thought was what lay beyond the veil in solemn silence, mysterious and foreboding.

Within so small an area enveloped in symbolism was mirrored eternal Majesty penetrating time: the embracing of opposing realms, the meeting of minds, the divine and the human. The Creator 'afar off' had condescended to 'tabernacle' among his chosen ones (John 1:14), desiring as David reminded Israel to be both Redeemer and Benefactor (Ps.103:1-5). Moses too: 'Know therefore that the Lord thy God, he is God, the faithful God, which keepeth covenant and mercy with them that love him and keep his commandments to a thousand generations' (Deut.7:9). It was a foretaste of heaven (Rev.21:3).

The ark illustrated this fact very clearly. If the exterior was resplendent with golden beauty, the venue where deity stooped to embrace humanity (Exod.25:22), the golden interior was not less worthy (Exod.25:11); the former a perpetual reminder of the great Jehovah's desire ('he is God') to share fellowship with his people ('which keepeth covenant and mercy'), the latter his promise to sustain them at all times ('the faithful God'). He not only redeems his elect, he also 'keeps' them (1 Peter 1:3-5), and the three items inside the precious box – manna within a golden pot (Exod.16), Aaron's rod of authority (Numb.17), and the moral law written upon tablets of stone (Deut.10:1-5; Heb.9:4) – revealed that truth.

THE TABLE IN THE WILDERNESS

With the history of his people in mind, the desert wanderings particularly, Solomon's father expressed an astonishing truth (one in a series revealed to him); namely, that God is a 'Father' to those who fear him (Ps.103:7,13,14). What a difficult concept to believe for his people who had witnessed the destruction of the mighty land of Egypt (Exod.7-12)! Such awesome and terrifying power, that could divide 'the depths' (Ps.106:9) and topple the mighty Pharaoh from his throne and bury him in sea water (Exod.14:28; Ps.136:15), was not something associated with 'fatherhood' (Rom. 9:17). Nor, when at Sinai, was exclusion from his immediate presence (Exod.19:12; Heb.12:20).

True the divine energy had been poured out on their behalf (Pss.78:12; 106:22), a remarkable condescension, but that in itself did not necessarily denote a paternal interest in them. In so short a period, they had cried out prayerfully to him from the depth of their sufferings (Exod.2:23), had in Moses been provided with a leader (Exod.4:29-31; Ps.105:26), and no doubt joyful yet in a daze (for they 'understood not thy wonders in Egypt', Pss.105:43; 106:7) had departed from their torment under the watchful eye of their enemies (Exod.3:21,22). But they were as sheep following the Shepherd (Ps.78: 52), not children their 'Father'.

Then, suddenly, the scene changed. The noise and bustle of the narrow streets of a great city were about six weeks travelling time to their rear (Exod.16:1), to which they could not return, and they were surrounded by the wide expanse of the silent and unknown desert. Security appeared to have surrendered to sand, victory over their enemies to vulnerability, and the sights and sounds of wrathful Sovereignty to that of frailty on their part. As promised, the wanderers had a plentiful supply of 'jewels of silver, and jewels of gold, and raiment', none of which could be eaten – and they were hungry (Exod.3:22; 16:3). If only faith could have spread as rapidly as panic! How lofty was God, how lowly was their need, and how far he would have to stoop to satisfy it! Making matters worse was the distress and disappointment the travellers had already experienced, when he appeared to have let them down. In fact, tantalised them. They had suffered the travail and concern of all desert wanderers, a great thirst under a burning sun. Thus, when an oasis was sighted, with what joy they hastened towards it, the breath shortening, the heart pounding, and the pace quickening the nearer they got to it. WATER

- yet undrinkable! They called it 'Marah' because it was bitter, and the experience equally so (Exod.15:23,24).

The people turned on Moses in anger; Moses turned to God in prayer, who supplied a miracle. Pure water was supplied, but from the peoples' point of view, not paternally, but obligatory: 'If thou wilt diligently hearken to the voice of the Lord thy God, and wilt do that which is right in his sight, and will give ear to his commandments, and keep all his statutes, I will put none of these diseases upon thee, which I have brought upon the Egyptians, for I am the Lord that healeth thee' (Exod.15:26). The lesson had been learned.

So, now they were hungry and panic-stricken. This time the nation's fury increased as its sin deepened. The cry ascended, and was cynical, 'Can God furnish a table in the wilderness? (Ps.78: 19)' Not only was God's servant once again the butt of the disillusioned peoples' anger, but Aaron the divinely appointed high priest too, and even God himself was slighted. After all he had accomplished for them, in rescuing the nation from oppression, the people resented it. Better to have died in Egypt, and 'by the hand of the Lord' too, than in the desert (Exod.16:2,3). Knowing how powerful was Jehovah, and what he had done to Pharaoh who also rebelled against him (Exod.5:2; Ps.136:15), the audacious former slaves were taking a risk, tempting Providence.

Yet despite this, something amazing occurred. David understood. Instead of almighty God pouring out his wrath in judgment upon his people because of their sin, he recognised their frailty – and pitied them, as a Father would. From the dust of the ground he had created them (Gen.2:7), and in the dust of the desert he fed them, filling his chosen people's 'mouth with good things' in order to renew them (Ps.103:5,13,14). But Jehovah is not a doting 'parent', who spoils his child, but One who expects obedience in return (Exod.16:4).

The result was yet another miracle. Each day the dawn exposed what Jehovah had supplied during the night, 'angel's food' covering the ground like dew (Ps.78:25). That is, apart from the Sabbath, the people having been supplied twice the usual provision of this heaven-sent 'bread' the previous morning (Exod. 16:5; Ps.105:40; John 6:31). Similar to coriander seed, small in size, round in shape and tasting 'like wafers made with honey' (Exod.16:14,31), this new item on the nation's menu might at first sight have appeared a frugal meal when compared with what Egypt could have supplied (Numb.11:4-7; Prov.23:2). In fact, it was 'manna', 'a portion' (Exod.16:15), but God's people never have need to envy those outside of his grace. What he supplies is always adequate to prevent even the hungriest from having to beg for more (Ps.37:1, 25; Phil.4:19). Besides, 'manna' was not the only item of the nation's diet. There was also a plentiful supply of 'feathered fowls' (Ps.78:27,28), blown to the encampment by the Creator of the winds, as plentiful as dust or 'the sand of the sea' (Exod.16:13; Numb.11:31).

And as this generous provision had arrived miraculously, it also departed in the same manner. The river Jordan crossed, the destination reached, Canaan's corn the new diet: the settlers awoke one morning to discover the ground free of the daily 'bread' (Matt. 6:11) they had been feeding upon for forty years (Exod.16: 35; Josh.5:12). Without this 'manna' (and the birds) they could not have survived; small wonder a segment of it was placed as a memorial inside the ark within the most holy place (Exod.16:33, 34), and appropriately in a golden pot (Heb.9:4).

BUDS, BLOSSOMS AND ALMONDS

Lying beside the pot was a staff, or perhaps part of one as the ark was small (Heb.9:4), the kind used by the patriarchs when walking long distances (Exod.4:2). It had once belonged to Aaron (Numb.17:3). If the 'manna' revealed Jehovah as a pitying Father, 'slow to anger, and plenteous in mercy' (Ps.103:8,13), the staff or rod was a constant reminder that accompanying his love was his undoubted sternness (Numb.16:35).

Seeking to control about a couple of a million people could not have been straightforward (Exod.12:37), particularly once they had got used to their new desert environment. During the 'romance' of the rescue from bondage how dependent they had been upon Moses, but after about a year restlessness rippled across the ranks.

It came in three stages. At first it might not have been surprising, in fact expected. The 'strangers' in the nation (Deut.10: 19; 29:11), the 'mixed multitude' (Exod.12:37) of Egyptian refugees who had fled from God's vengeance upon their country (Exod.7-12), expressed their dissatisfaction with desert life, and also with God's daily provision of the 'manna'. This open rebellion spread to other sections of the nation (Numb.11:4,5). Moses was understandably alarmed and brought the matter to the Lord. It was an historic moment, because the result was the establishing of the first Israelite 'Parliament' ('Sanhedrin'), consisting of seventy men 'plus two' (Numb.11:16-26).

But the divisive spirit was not confined to the ordinary people; it could even be found within Moses' immediate family, in fact his brother and sister, and ironically the dispute between the siblings also concerned a 'stranger'. Aaron and Miriam (Exod.2:7; 4:14; 15:20) objected to Moses having married again (Exod.2:21), this time to an Ethiopian woman, a Cushite, whose ancestry incidentally had introduced idolatry into the world (Gen.10:6-8; Numb.12:1). Also, as noted earlier (Chapter two), if the minority view is accepted that Sheba had travelled to Jerusalem not from Arabia but from Egypt, then Moses' new wife was one of Sheba's ancestors! It is unlikely though.

But the family dispute concerned much more than their brother's choice of a wife. Moses was the nation's leader, appointed by God, and he was younger than they were (Exod.2:4.7; 6:20). Behind the façade of righteous indignation therefore probably lay the spirit of jealousy, exposed in their challenge to their brother: 'Hath the Lord indeed spoken only to Moses? Hath he not spoken also by US (Numb.12:2)?'

It was not however that which incurred God's anger - and it was directed primarily at Miriam who appears to have encouraged Aaron (a weak character, Exod.32:1,2) - but rather the rebelliousness of their spirit. Unlike their brother, they had not proved faithful (Numb.12:7). In opposing him, even though he was closely related, they had wilfully alienated themselves from the will of God.

The judgment was severe; Miriam the prime culprit struck down with leprosy (Numb.12:10), and Aaron having to watch her suffer as he submitted to his brother's authority in calling him 'lord', pleading for forgiveness and their sister's healing. Moses in turn pleaded with God, but the severity of the judgment reflected God's displeasure when rebellion leaps within the human heart (Col.1:21). Miriam, despite the fact that she was a prophetess and the leader of the women (Exod.15:20) as well as the sister of the nation's hero, was nevertheless banished from the encampment for a week (Numb.12:9-15).

Rebellion also marked the third stage of the general restlessness, but this time it was much more alarming, so severe in fact the entire nation was under threat. It was not about food, or even a private family squabble however serious its nature, but rather an open challenge to Moses as Israel's leader and Aaron as its high priest. Nor was the challenge conducted by one or two individuals, or by an inconsequential group, but by three men backed by 250 of Israel's tribal leaders 'famous in the congregation, men of renown'. As such, they were numbered among Moses' most intimate circle, his 'privy council'. He had cause to fall on his face before God in prayer (Numb.1:1-16; 16:2-4).

The three instigators, Korah, Dathan and Abiram (whose infamous names have gone down in Israel's history) are also not without interest (Numb.16:1). Korah (Jude 11), of the tribe of Levi, was through his father a grandson of Kohath (Exod.6:16) whose descendants were now responsible for the care of the tabernacle's holy vessels and furniture (Numb.3:27,28; 4:17-20). The other two were from the tribe of Reuben, whose progenitor was also guilty of sinful mischief, and was sternly told by his father Jacob he was 'unstable as water' and would not succeed (Gen.49:4). But would Dathan and Abiram?

The argument presented by the rebels was on three levels: first, the nation should be governed democratically, secondly, everyone within it should be considered as having shared equally in the grace of God. That being so, thirdly, the leaders have no more authority in the nation than anyone else (Numb.16:3). The debate has continued in the Church throughout the generations since. But behind the reasoning lay humanistic as well as tribal motives; God opposed by man, and the tribe of Levi by that of Reuben and the rest.

Since the fall of mankind (Gen.3), heaven's prerogative to choose whatever and whoever suits the divine programme has always instinctively rankled sinners (Rom.9:15-23), even many of them among the elect. God showing mercy to whom he wills (Exod.33:19), selecting a minority to serve him (Exod.24:1-11), favouring some at the expense of others (2 Tim.2:20): these evidences of God's sovereignty have always met with an unfavourable response.

Like Lucifer in eternity past (Is.14:12-15), man by nature seeks elevation not submission. Therefore, should not every one within the 'holy nation' (Deut.7:6; 1 Peter 2:9) be eligible for leadership, and elected democratically to this high office? Thus, the charge levelled at Moses and Aaron: 'wherefore then lift ye up yourselves above the congregation of the Lord (Numb.16:3)?' The rebels mentioned Jehovah, but conveniently overlooked the fact that Moses and Aaron had not selected themselves for leadership, God did, and their knowledge of his name ('I AM') and something of Israel's history ('The Lord God of your fathers…') had demonstrated the fact a year or so earlier (Exod.3:13-16).

Then the argument continued: there was no difference between the leadership and every individual in the nation ('ALL the congregation are holy, everyone of them, and the Lord is among them', Numb.16:3). Had not Jehovah called them ALL a 'holy people' (Deut.7:6), were they therefore not ALL citizens of a 'holy nation' (1 Peter 2:9), and was not the presence of the tabernacle the sign that he was in the midst of them ALL? In which case, should they not ALL have an opportunity to lead the nation? But the rebels had deliberately overlooked the presence of the 'strangers' living alongside them (Deut.10:19), a people who were certainly not considered equal to their Israelite neighbours, barred from observing the Passover (Exod.12:43) and just tolerated as refugees (Deut.29:11). As for the Israelites themselves: evidently Korah and his associates were unaware of the two levels to be considered, the racial as well as the spiritual. The nation of Israel, apart from the 'strangers', consisted of citizens all of whom were related RACIALLY to Abraham (Gen.12:1-3), but did they all share the same intensity of faith, were therefore SPIRITUALLY related to the great Patriarch (Gal.3:7)? As a famous 'Hebrew of the Hebrews' (Phil.3:3) would state centuries later, 'For they are not all Israel, which are of Israel' (Rom.9:6).

But behind the open rebellion were other considerations, more easily detectable, concerning rivalries between priests and Levites (Numb.16:8-11) and those that were inter-tribal. The Israelite priesthood had been divinely established through Aaron and his immediate family (Exod.28:1, 'and no man taketh this honour unto himself, but he that is called of God, as was Aaron (Heb.5:4).'

By contrast, the remainder of Levi's descendants (Exod.6: 16-10) although privileged by God to be brought 'near to himself' as Moses pointed out to Korah (Numb.16:9), nevertheless only SUPPORTED the priests in performing the menial tasks in the tabernacle. While the priests ministered at the altar of burnt offering and within the sanctuary, Aaron even permitted to enter the 'Holiest of all' once a year (Heb.9:3), Korah and his fellow Kohathites were obliged to carry the golden vessels, including the heavy ark of the covenant (Numb.4:15). His rebellion therefore was the result of envy. Korah though was shrewd. Having opposed Aaron, he now turned upon Moses. To do this, and to make the rebellion more appealing, he widened its scope by encouraging Dathan and Abiram to join him. Being Reubenites, they too were envious, with a quarrel to match the Kohathites. Why was Moses the nation's leader? He was a descendant of Levi (Exod.2:1-10; 6:20), Jacob's third son, but Reuben was the firstborn (Gen.29:32-34). Jacob had referred to him as 'the excellency of dignity, and the excellency of power' (Gen.49:3). True, but he was also described by his father as 'unstable as water', although Levi was worse, an 'instrument of cruelty' (Gen.49:3-6)! It was however conveniently overlooked that Reuben had forfeited his father's blessing. According to the practice at the time, in having a sexual relationship with his father's concubine (Gen. 35:22), he was seeking to usurp his father's authority within the family unit. As a result, the 'blessing' of the 'firstborn' was bestowed upon Joseph's two sons Ephraim and Manasseh (Gen.48: 5). Incidentally, Sheba may also have heard that Solomon's step-brother sinned in the same way as Reuben (2 Sam.16:22).

In any other community the rebels' arguments might have had substance, but the travellers to the land of promise were not citizens of an ordinary nation. They were subjects of a theocracy not a democracy (as are members of the Christian Church), recipients of covenantal grace whose pathway was strewn with miracles. As Moses reminded them, 'who is there of all flesh' that had seen the greatness and the glory of the living God, had actually heard his voice – and LIVED (Deut. 5:24-26)? The 253 men knew this, but were prepared to barter the blessings for personal ambition (Numb.16:1-4), and so insensitive had they become in their stubbornness, the nation's immediate history had been forgotten. Pharaoh had also opposed Moses' God-appointed leadership (Exod.5:2), and upon reflection they would have remembered what had become of HIM (Exod.14:28; Ps.136:15)!

Having challenged Moses and Aaron, what did Korah and his supporters expect the brothers to do about the situation? Had they agreed with their challengers, and surrendered their distinctive roles (an action that needless to say nobody considered), how shocked the rebels would have been. Instead, in this moment of crisis, Moses revealed the meekness for which he was noted (Numb.12:3). He listened to the accusations, but remained silent (Prov.14:29), walked away, and prayed. His opponents would not have expected him to do otherwise (Numb.14:5; 16:4), but their open challenge indicated they were confident Jehovah would understand their grievances.

Moses returned, the Lord had decided upon the matter, and the 'bluff' had been called. How Korah and his supporters felt when they heard the news is unknown, but the message was both challenging and daring. Perhaps, even alarming. Were he and his followers dissatisfied with being Levites, and believed they should be entitled to perform priestly duties? Well they would, like real priests, first thing in the morning (Exod.30:7)! Whether exhilarated or nervous at the prospect when Moses threw their challenge back at them ('Ye take too much upon you'), they must have felt an ominous sting in his remark (Numb.16:3,7).

Immediately, three thoughts must have sprung to Korah's mind and that of his followers. To begin with, it was one thing to feel cheated of the priesthood, but another to exercise it, particularly as they had not been trained to do so. And what if they made a mistake, or were considered unworthy in the sight of God? Nadab and Abihu were carried dead from the holy place because they offered 'strange fire before the Lord' (Lev. 10:1-7) - and they were REAL priests!

Again, what would happen the following morning if Moses and Aaron were vindicated? Not only would they in challenging his servants have questioned God himself, but treated their own calling as Levites contemptuously – as a 'small thing' (Numb.16:8-11). The rebellious Levites must surely have retired for the night uneasily, and they had every cause to do so.

Whatever the rebels believed would happen to them if they failed to achieve their aims – sickness, banishment (Numb.12:10, 15), alienation from God (Numb.14:42), stoning (Numb.15:32-36) – nothing could have prepared them for the drama of what occurred throughout the encampment the next day (Numb.16). It was the most catastrophic occasion since heaven's judgments upon the Egyptians (Exod.7-12), but this time it was the turn of the Israelites to experience the intense heat of wrathful displeasure. It cascaded over the nation in a terrifying display of retribution, directed from heaven and through nature (Matt.11:25). By the close of the day the three ringleaders, their families, and the 250 other malcontents were dead (Jude 11); flames of fury had engulfed some, and the quaking ground had buried the rest (Numb.16:32,35).

The dust had hardly settled, or the smoke cleared, when God returned to the subject again (Numb.17). This time the emphasis was not upon Moses, but rather upon his brother Aaron. The people had already learned, through the establishing of the sanctuary, how vital was the need for one to intercede for them before so holy a Deity (Lev.16:17; 1 Tim.2:5). The role of high priest, with a calling rooted in heaven and not upon earth (Heb.5:4), was therefore at the heart of the nation's life. Yet Aaron's sanctified position had been challenged in a most alarming way, and with it the role itself, resulting in the wrathful terror recently inflicted. Every tent contained a trembling family (Numb.16:34).

The dozens of rebels therefore having been dealt with, the matter had to be established once and for all, although the Israelites having been travelling for a year it was an indictment upon them that the lesson had to be re-learned (Numb.14:34). Apparently, such was their sin, it was not sufficient for them to trust God's Word alone (Exod.28:38), so 'dull of hearing' were they (Heb.5: 11) nothing less than a miracle would impress them. Besides, although the rebels were dead, their revolt had to be remembered as a warning (Numb.17:10).

At God's command therefore twelve staffs (rods) were offered to Moses, one from each of the tribal leaders, and upon each staff he inscribed the name of the tribe it represented. Then a thirteenth staff was produced, for 'Levi', as this special tribe was separated from the others because it belonged uniquely to God (Numb.1:49,50). It bore Aaron's name. The thirteen staffs were then placed side by side within the sanctuary 'before the testimony' (Numb.17:4), and because Moses was not permitted to enter the most holy place that meant as close to the veil as possible.

By the following morning, the rod inscribed with Aaron's name had as promised undergone a miraculous transformation. The plain wooden staff had blossomed with buds and almonds (Numb. 17:5,8; Zech.6:12); not for the last time, the living God had produced life from that which had been 'dead' (John 5:21,26), and as a result had claimed it as his own (Numb.17:10; Ephes.2:1-6).

There was no mistaking the choice God had made, although a simple trust in his Word would and should have proved sufficient (Exod.28:1). Thus, inside the most holy place a section of Aaron's inscribed rod was placed within the ark (Heb.9:4), as a permanent reminder of the authority invested in him (Heb.4:14-16; 12:2). He, and he alone, was indeed the true high priest (Heb.5:4,5), and within his immediate family the high priestly succession would be harboured (Numb.20:23-29).

THE FINGER OF GOD

There was a third item within the covenantal ark: two tablets of stone upon which were written, with Jehovah's own hand (Exod. 34:1), both halves of the moral law (Deut.10:2,5), as noted earlier (Chapter nine) the sinner's duty first to God and then to his neighbour (Deut.6:5; Matt.22:37-39). God's miraculous provision was the connection between the three: the heavenly bread (Exod. 16), the blossoming staff (Numb.17) – and now the authoritative Law (Exod.20).

A closer examination of these three items reveals their relationship to each other on a deeper level, and why (at least, in the tabernacle, 1 Kings 8:9) they accompanied each other within the heart of the ark (Heb.9:4), immediately beneath the sacred area where two realms met (Exod.25:22), heaven and humanity. They symbolised one of the most profound of all mysteries, that time is the object of eternity's interest (Is.40:25-31), the world the subject of the Creator's love, the elect the few the Father seeks to worship him (John 3:16; 4:23).

Time means everything to man. He is controlled, and limited by it. The mere mention of day and night signifies its importance to him (Gen.1:14). However, eternity overshadows time. At its heart stands the throne, and upon it sits almighty God (Rev.4:2-5). He is ablaze with glory; the pivot around which all existence revolves, and the focal point for all thanksgiving and praise. It is his sovereign right to exercise ultimate power in every centimetre of his universe, his gracious delight to reserve judgment and distribute mercy where he desires (Exod.33:19).

To God, man imprisoned within the framework of time appears only as a 'grasshopper' (Is. 40:22). Once crowned by his Creator with glory and honour (Ps.8:5) and sharing sweet fellowship with him (Gen.2), in Eden as we have seen man plunged to the depths in disgrace and was driven out, angelic beings wielding swords of fire preventing a return (Gen.3:17-24). So estranged from God, the Source from which he came (Gen.2:7), man feels no sense of loss, no unease. That is, until the flames of hell smother him everlastingly (Mark 9:43). Those stone tablets inscribed with the holy law therefore revealed not just the righteous God's awesome character, but also his love for the elect among the creatures of time (1 John 4:10). His bursting forth upon Sinai from the realm of glory accompanied by myriads of angels (Deut.33:2; Jude 14), was a fearful spectacle (Heb.12:19-21), but it was also a gracious act. Heaven was refusing to desert humanity, leaving it to perish in the mire of eternal damnation. There in the depths helpless and hope-less lay the remnant of the 'everlastingly loved' (Jer.31:3), the elect, and they had to be rescued. God 'so loved the world' (John 3:16), because that is where they were to be found.

But the tablets were also a reminder, that for reconciliation to be achieved, two factors had to be considered: the character of God (Is.6:1-3), whose initiative it was (Exod.33:19), and the plight of the elect (Ephes.2:1). Heaven's perfection and humanity's corruption could never embrace, even when divine love was present; it is irresistible (John 6:44,65), but not superficial. A paradox was demanded. God had first to frown before he could smile: the elect, broken over the 'wheel' of tender mercy, before being embraced by grace.

Thus the Law was presented, ten 'nails' hammered into the pride and conscience of man (Exod.20:1-17), revealing the stark reality of naked truth; that God is more pure than the individual could imagine, and the individual is more corrupt than personal belief will admit. Only grace can supply that understanding (John 16:13) and the ability to weep for mercy (Rom.7:24,25) - hell awaiting those without the gift (John 16:8) - yet nothing can be more painful to the soul.

It was about heaven's concern for the redemption of the elect, the 'Israel of God' (Gal.6:16), that when Korah revolted the Israelites experienced the brunt of a terrible indignation (Numb.16-17). In opposing God's appointed high priest and the high priestly succession (Exod.28:1), he had not only violated the will of God, but had also undervalued the moral law. The latter (the stone tablets) and the office of high priest (the blossoming rod) combined to direct sinners to the only Redeemer (who years later would be referred to as 'THE BRANCH', Zech.6:12); on the one hand, the convicted soul seeking refuge in him (Gal.3:24; Heb.6:18), and on the other, receiving assurance of it (1 Tim.2:5; Heb.12: 2).

Left to itself the moral law reflecting absolute purity can only condemn the sinner, not redeem him (Rom.7:9-14; 8:3). The high priest's role, representing God before sinners and sinners at the bar of judgment (Zech.3:1-5), is to intercede (Heb.4:24-26). In him, symbolised by the stench from the sacrificial offerings, sins are dealt a final blow; in him, the sweet scent of incense in which he was swathed as he entered the most holy place, symbolised the elect attired in the whiteness of heaven's purity (Zech.3:4; Rev.19: 14). Thus, years later, a prophet would speak of the King-priest (Zech.6:13), as

'OUR RIGHTEOUSNESS' (Jer.23:6).

However, God not only redeems his favoured, providing a 'raiment' of purity for each of them (Zech.3:4), the golden pot of 'angel's food' (Ps.78:25) was a perpetual reminder of his promise to supply their daily need throughout the forty years of the wilderness wanderings (Exod.16:32,33) - and also something even more remarkable. As the tablets foreshadowed the One who would 'fulfil the law' (Matt.17:5), and the blossoming rod the forthcoming 'Branch' (Zech.6:12), the pieces of manna in the pot ('bread of heaven', Ps.105:40) anticipated the spiritual nourishment that would sustain the elect (1 Peter 1:5); the 'Bread' of God descending from heaven to the world bringing eternal life with him, with which they would be everlastingly 'nourished' (John 6: 31-35; 17:3).

WITHIN TOUCHING DISTANCE

The ark had now been reached (Heb.4:15,16). Between the golden cherubim standing like sentinels, their wings spread across the mercy seat (Exod.25:19,20), could be seen the dazzling cloud radiating the glory of God. The atmosphere within the most holy place was heavy with billowing incense vapour, and thick with the sweetness of its scent. Jehovah was about to commune with his servant Aaron (Exod.25:22), who must have felt the most solitary figure on earth.

His duties that special day of atonement ('Yom Kippur') were on behalf of the nation, each tribe represented by the twelve precious stones of differing colours upon the square of multi-coloured cloth (the 'breastplate') he wore (Exod.28:15-21). In other words, as he stood before the ark each Israelite vicariously stood with him. But this was not only a solitary moment, but also a private one: it was reserved first of all for the confession of his own sins.

He could not have felt more unworthy, standing alone with the burden of the entire nation upon his shoulders, an onyx stone resting on each one inscribed with the names of six tribes (Exod. 28:9,10). Thoughts of his two sons, whose unworthy behaviour was punished by death (Lev.10:1-7), must surely have sprung to mind; thoughts too of his own lapses from godly behaviour, when his brother was obliged to castigate him for his sinfulness (Exod. 32:21). How worthy of death and divine retribution was he, how sinful, and shame-faced! Yet, the solution to his understandable grief was close at hand. Heaven was at that moment as filled with his prayers, as he was enveloped with incense; prayers for mercy and forgiveness, mingled with those of thanksgiving (Lev.16:13). It was customary (Rev.8:4). But he knew his pleading would have been in vain, apart from the bowl he held, into which blood had been poured. The maxim was well known (Heb.9:22), recorded for posterity: 'it is the blood that maketh an atonement for the soul' (Lev.17:11).

He understood the ceremonial law (Lev.16:14), and therefore dipping his finger in the blood he sprinkled the mercy seat the appropriate SEVEN times (Gen.1:31). Had he not done so, the burning brilliance of the glory Aaron was witnessing as it hovered over the mercy seat could not have been endured (Rev.4:5). His brother had experienced its overwhelming presence (Exod.40:35), as had the priests that Solomon knew, who had been rendered incapable of remaining on their feet (1 Kings 8:10,11).

But the blood of the sacrifice had been applied: heaven had 'communed' with humanity (Exod.25:22), God with sinners; mercy and truth had met each other; righteousness and peace had 'kissed' (Ps.85:10) - almighty God was appeased, and Aaron was calm, trusting in the immutable promise that he had been forgiven, and his sins dealt with (Heb.6:18).

SECTION
THREE

'...mount Moriah, where the Lord appeared unto David...'
(2 Chron. 3:1)

TWELVE
A Great While to Come

There surely is little doubt - a view taken in this book - that in her quest Sheba's thoughts would have been directed by Solomon to the most obvious location, the epicentre of the Israelite's life and the nation's existence: Mount Moriah, and the altars that were erected there at different periods of time, both of which were of great significance. Abraham built the first (Gen.22:1-9), and Jerusalem's temple with which Solomon was associated contained the second (1 Kings 8:64); an altar arising from the one used during the desert travelling. But not long before the temple was built another altar had featured in Israel's history, and as Solomon's father was involved how could his son have resisted relating the story to Sheba? It was a period of great sorrow and trauma. David (1012-972BC) had incurred God's anger by commanding his general to count his subjects. As a consequence, 70,000 of them were struck down in judgment (2 Sam.24:1,15). Sheba may have been shocked to learn this, and questioned why God had taken such drastic action. Is it not the shepherd's responsibility to know how many sheep are in his flock, or a monarch's to register the citizens of his kingdom? Perhaps Solomon had told Sheba that the Creator knows the stars in the firmament by name (Ps.147:4), as well as the name of each of his elect (Matt.10:30). Besides, on two separate occasions Moses counted the people (Exod.30:12; Numb.1:2).

But Moses had received his instructions from God for practical reasons; David acted arbitrarily with questionable motives, pride rather than faith and spirituality being the deciding factor. Later his son would write, 'Pride goeth before destruction, and an haughty spirit before a fall' (Prov.16:18). So it proved to be for David, if not destruction, certainly his peoples' 'fall' (2 Sam. 24:10).

How contrasting were the ways of the King, and the way of the king, the vertical as opposed to the horizontal. Abraham had been told by God to gaze UPWARDS and attempt the impossible, to count the stars ('so shall thy seed be'); Joab commanded by David to look OUTWARDS and number the people (2 Sam.24:9). How encouraged the Patriarch was in the words of his Lord (Gen. 15:5), but David sought as great an encouragement in the words of his general (2 Sam.24:2).

Yet in doing so, David's pride having clouded his faith, two very important matters were deliberately overlooked. First was the wonder of that remarkable promise made to Abraham, so remarkable in fact it was repeated several times lest astonishment should prevent the Patriarch from taking it in, that from him would multitudes arise; as many as the earth's dust, the firmament's stars, or the sand's grain (Gen.13:6; 15:5; 22:17). Did the old man require any more metaphors to describe the immensity of the blessing, and how innumerable would the company be (Rev.7:9)?

Then again, had David forgotten the promise or believed the centuries had evaporated it; did he need to assure himself of its validity? Whatever the reason, he had committed a great sin, insulting his Lord and disregarding the major rule in the life of faith, to trust God's Word (Gen.3:1-4).

When David realised what he had done he sought forgiveness from God, whose judgment was at least tempered with mercy. David was given a choice from three options, each one of which would cause suffering to him and his people. Having to decide for his subjects was a punishment in itself: seven YEARS of famine (starvation and death), three MONTHS of enemy oppression (humiliation and death), or three DAYS of pestilence (disease and death). David chose the latter, and he suffered the anguish of learning that as a result of his sin – although he was spared – 70,000 within the nation perished (2 Sam.24:13-15).

The angel of death was then about to destroy the entire city of Jerusalem, but God restrained his judgment when he saw David had been brought to abject submission and repentance (2 Sam.24: 16). Earlier in the presence of God, although he believed he had 'sinned greatly', David considered his disregard of God's promise to Abraham in having the people counted merely a 'foolish' act. Now though, with Jerusalem threatened and so many of his people dead he had been brought even lower; 'foolishness' had given way to 'wickedness' (2 Sam.24:10,17). David had learned a valuable lesson, that true repentance chooses its words very carefully.

On the temple mount, at the instructions of the prophet Gad, David had sought out the owner of a local threshing floor, Araunah (Ornan) by name (2 Sam.24:18; 2 Chron.3:1). To the man's undoubted surprise, his sovereign offered to buy the threshing floor as a suitable place for the erection of an altar. At first, Araunah was prepared to freely give his king not only the premises, but also his oxen for the sacrifice, as well as wood for the fire. David, no doubt moved by the gesture of his loyal subject (were any of Araunah's family affected by the pestilence?), insisted upon paying. A transaction was made, fifty shekels of silver, a king's ransom to Araunah. So another altar was built on Mount Moriah, a burnt offering of oxen offered upon it in order to appease God, and the judgment passed (2 Sam.24:25).

However, not long before that incident occurred David received some astonishing news, so remarkable, it is equally astonishing that having done so he allowed himself to openly sin against God.

CONFIDANT OF THE KING

David had a son called Nathan (2 Sam.5:14), Solomon's sibling (1 Chron.3:5), and although the name was popular in Israel, it may have been that he was given it in honour of the prophet. Whatever the truth of the matter, Nathan was certainly a close friend of his

king, which was just as well when the accusing finger had to be
pointed ('Thou art the man') over David's immoral involvement with
Bathsheba (2 Sam.12:1-7). Again, only one who moved comfortably
in royal circles could have gained access to her so easily when David
lay dying, to warn her of Adonijah's attempt to gain the throne (1
Kings 1:11,12).

Nathan then was highly respected, both within David's court
and also in the land as a whole, being very able in spiritual as well as
in literary matters (1 Chron.29:29; 2 Chron.9:29). He was practical
too, whose advice David sought in the reorganisation of the Levites
(2 Chron.29:25).

A FAMILIAR TECHNIQUE

One day at the height of David's powers, a period of tranquillity
following years of warfare (2 Sam.7:1), as mentioned earlier (Chapter
seven), Nathan visited him. Visits from God's servant were
infrequent, but when Nathan appeared the King knew he had to listen
well. This particular occasion though proved to be so extraordinary,
God's message so startling, David felt the need to remain seated
when prayerfully contemplating it (2 Sam.7:18).

When he had seen Nathan approaching, with a prophet's solemn
step and penetrating gaze, David probably suspected from Nathan's
demeanour that the desire to have the temple built during his reign
had been rejected by God. Affirmation is invariably swift to be made
known, on this occasion though disappointment was in the air, and
confirmed when in place of the nod of approval Nathan's message
opened with the supplementary 'encouragements' - God's favour
toward David, his rise from shepherd boy to mighty king, and the
protection he received on his way to eminence (2 Sam.7:8,9) – usually
associated with an ultimately negative response.

Nathan delivered God's word in measured tones in no hurry to
reach the enthralling climax. Despite being a close friend, his task
was to present the message as God had revealed it to him, and not
like the false prophets, selecting that portion most likely to please
the king (2 Chron.18:5). Thus, David had to wait while Nathan skirted

the periphery of the message before introducing the 'key' to the understanding of the revelation; just two words, 'for ever' (2 Sam.7:13).

David had guessed correctly; he would not be building the temple (1 Chron.17:4), in fact (and how bitterly disappointed he must have been to hear the news) he would not even live to see it in its completed glory (1 Kings 8:15). After his death his 'seed', one of his sons, would receive that honour (1 Chron.29:19), but how strange the son's name was not mentioned (2 Sam.7:12). At a later date, David promised Bathsheba their son Solomon would succeed him (1 Kings 1:17), but he was not the eldest (2 Sam.3: 2-5; 5:14), the natural heir apparent, and an older sibling claimed that privilege (1 Kings 1:5). Thus, the pathway to the throne was strewn with uncertainties, and therefore on the day of Nathan's visit neither of the men could be completely sure who was being referred to in the revelation.

But very soon, it became clear why David's successor had not been mentioned by name; there was no reason to do so, because his building of the temple was not the most important aspect of the message after all. In fact, nor was the temple itself! To David's undoubted surprise, the emphasis had suddenly changed, from the erection of the temple to the establishing of the throne (2 Sam.7: 13). Then David became aware of what was happening. Nathan was employing the methodology familiar to all prophets, when short and long-term prophecies overlapped each other. To the untrained ear the approach is confusing, because two subjects were being referred to at the same time.

The reason for this technique was practical, to assure the listeners of the prophecy's validity; that if it was fulfilled in the short-term, was the prophet's long-term prediction not also likely to be correct? Jesus the Prophet, used this method when in a famous discourse the subjects of Jerusalem's fall and the second advent overlap (Mark 13); if the latter was well beyond his listeners' day, the former would be fulfilled within the lifetime of most present. As an historical fact, nearly forty years later (70AD) Titus notoriously laid siege to the city, preventing escape by surrounding it with a 'trench' (Luke 19:43). That being so, is not the second advent a future reality?

The first part of Nathan's message was straightforward: 'And when thy days be fulfilled, and thou shalt sleep with thy fathers, I will set up thy seed after thee, which shall proceed out of thy bowels, and I will establish his kingdom. He shall build an house for my name...' Clearly, Solomon was inferred. But David, being a prophet himself, was familiar with the technique having used it in the compositions of his psalms (e.g. 2; 16; 22; 40; 110 etc). He was therefore not confused when the subject matter became more complex: '......and I will stablish the throne of his kingdom FOR EVER' (2 Sam.7:12, 13). Suddenly Nathan had introduced a new concept, directing David's attention from the temporal to the eternal, from the temple to the throne.

STRONGER THAN CEDAR

David would have been swift to notice the irony in Nathan's message from the Lord. Shortly before, he had made his desire known to the prophet to have God's house built. After all, he reminded Nathan, he lived in a house of cedar, but the ark of God dwelt merely 'within curtains' (2 Sam.7:2). The Lord though hearing thoughts 'afar off', as David knew only too well (Ps.139: 2), turned the sincere ambition for God's glory into a divine ambition for the glory of David's lineage: '.....the Lord telleth thee that he will make THEE a house. (2 Sam.7:11)'

In short, there was a further example of the prophet's art, the 'play' upon words (e.g. Numb.24:17; Is.7:14;8:1-8; Matt.16:18). First, the word 'house': what had begun as a message about building the temple (God's house) had developed into a remarkable prophecy concerning David's lineage (David's 'house'). Then in an example of short and long-term prophecies, the word 'seed': said Nathan, after David's passing his 'seed' (his son) would be raised up, who during his reign over an established kingdom would build God's 'house' (the temple). But a 'seed' from David's family (the Messiah), whose kingdom will be established FOR EVER, would also build the 'house' of the Lord (2 Sam.7:12,13); the Church, the 'holy temple' (John 2:19; Ephes.2:20), the 'house' he is still building (Matt.16:18). The climax of the message continued in the same vein, the use of the prophet's method, but this time with a 'play' upon relationships rather than words. David would have had no difficulty in understanding the nuances: 'I will be his father, and he shall be my son. If he commit iniquity, I will chasten him with the rod of men, and with the stripes of the children of men. But my mercy shall not depart away from him, as I took it from Saul, whom I put away before thee. (2 Sam.7:14)'

David was obviously comforted upon hearing of God's gracious promise to keep a 'fatherly eye' upon his son soon to succeed him as king (1 Chron.29:19). Of all people, David recognised the caring aspect of God's nature (Ps.103:13). Yet, soon after Sheba's visit, Solomon gave cause to be chastened, when through disobedience to Moses' warning and God's command (Deut.17:17) he married numerous heathen women, turning his nation into a 'multi-faith' society (1 Kings 11:1-13). The 'rod of men' was soon in action as the rebel Jeroboam attracted ten of the tribes to his side, leaving only the tribes of Judah and Benjamin loyal to Solomon's son Rehoboam (932-915BC). But for God's mercy as promised (2 Sam.7:14) on account of his 'royal covenant' with David (Ps.89:3), the situation would have been terminally catastrophic: nothing less than the death of the nation (1 Kings 12:1-19).

The 'father' and 'son' relationship was central to the preservation of David's 'house', the royal tribe of Judah, from which Jacob foretold 'Shiloh' would appear (Gen.49:10). In Joshua's day, Shiloh was the 'home' of the tabernacle where stood the ark of the covenant (Josh.18:1), thus the patriarch's prophecy was messianic, and therefore too vital for Satan to ignore. He attempted to destroy the 'house of David' and the royal line that emanated from it.

The seeds were sown during Solomon's reign (1 Kings 11:1-11) and grew to alarming proportions, as just mentioned, when his son Rehoboam took over the kingdom (1 Kings 11-12). But two kings later the situation exploded. King Jehoshaphat (873-849BC) 'joined affinity' with Ahab (875-854bc) the wicked king of the northern kingdom of Israel (2 Chron.18:1), whose queen was the notorious Jezebel (1 Kings 16:31). This political union eventually led to the marriage of Jehoshaphat's son and their daughter Athaliah who shared her parents' wickedness.

What a dark day therefore it was for the messianic message when, because of Jehoshaphat's folly, Athaliah left the palace on the hill in Samaria (1 Kings 16:24) and resided in Judah as Queen Consort (845-839BC), later Queen Mother, and then when her son Ahaziah was killed, Queen Dowager (2 Kings 8:16-18; 11:1-3). Not long before the southern kingdom of Judah had been 'strengthened' against Israel (2 Chron.17:1), and now Ahab and Jezebel's daughter sat in regal splendour in Jerusalem. How strange this must have seemed to the senior citizens of Judea, who remembered when Ahab and his family were their enemies. The sages would have shaken their heads in disbelief and suggested they still were.

So it proved to be. Through Athaliah, Satan attempted to thwart God's purposes by making Nathan's prophecy null and void. She set about to eradicate 'all the seed royal', and almost succeeded (2 Kings 11:1). Astonishingly, this even included the slaying of her own grandchildren.

Every prophecy breathed out by God is certain to be fulfilled (Is.55:11), and therefore Athaliah's evil intention to destroy the royal line of David were overshadowed by the safe hands of Providence. Seven-year-old Jehoash (Joash) – not Joash (Jehoash) of Israel in the north (2 Kings 13:10)! – the son of Ahaziah, was hidden from the butchery and the 'seed royal' lived on (2 Kings 11: 2,12).

But Satan waited patiently for the Messiah to arrive (Rev.12: 4), and then tried again to prevent Christ from reaching Calvary, where it was determined that he should fulfil Nathan's prophecy, that the 'seed of David' would be chastened with 'the stripes of the children of men' (2 Sam.7:14). First as an infant (Matt.2:16), then at the outset of his ministry (Luke 4:29), through his enemies (John 11:49-51), and even his friends (Matt.16:21-23). Had Athaliah succeeded, Jesus being of 'the tribe of Judah' (Rev.5:5), the 'fulness of the time' could not have arrived (Gal.4:4); the incarnation unable to take place, and all that would have meant in terms of the loss of everlasting hope.

But the 'father' and 'son' relationship was also pivotal in the foundation of the 'holy temple' of the Christian Church built by the Messiah (Ephes.2:20). He had stood in the Jordan waters at his baptism – the public commitment to the ministry given him by the

Father (John 17:4) - and everyone at the scene distinctly heard the voice from heaven, 'This is my beloved Son, in whom I am well pleased. (Matt.3:17)' It was an expression of 'delight' (Prov.8:30) to be heard again (Matt.17:5).

For those who had an 'eye' for the truth, everything about this extraordinary Figure - named 'Jesus' by heaven's decree (Matt.1:21) - would have reminded them of David, the subject of bedtime stories, and the role-model for the nation's youth (1 Sam. 17). True, unlike David, the battles Jesus fought were not military (they were more fierce than that), but were spiritual and verbal (e.g. Matt.4:1-11; John 5-8), nevertheless his credentials underlined the fact that he was the One for which Israel had been waiting for many centuries.

Bethlehem - 'the house of bread' (Ps.37:25; John 6:33-35) -was their birthplace (1 Sam.16:1; Luke 2:4) and both became shepherds, David the boy shepherd (1 Sam.16:11), and Jesus the good shepherd (Ezek.34:11,12), the one of sheep and the other of people (Is.40:11; John 10:11,14). It was from this 'little town' that revelation informed Israel the Ruler would come - 'David' by name, a 'prince' among his people (Ezek.34:24) – who, unlike the national hero, was 'from everlasting' (Mic.5:2).

Glory (John 17:24) was all this 'seed of David' had known (Acts 13:22,23; Rom.1:3). Heaven's eternal wealth was his (2 Cor. 8:9), but poverty awaited him (Lev.1: 14; Luke 2:24); a poor virgin his mother (Is.7:14; Luke 1:48), a lowly stable the 'delivery suite', a feeding trough his first resting place (Luke 2:12,16) – yet a prosperous and just King, a descendant of David the king, 'THE LORD OUR RIGHTEOUSNESS' (Jer.23:5,6).

MORE BEAUTIFUL THAN LILIES

Solomon was privileged to reign over Israel during the nation's greatest period in history (chapter one), when his renowned sagacity was widespread, 'all kingdoms' were subservient to him, 'riches and honour' were his in abundance, and the people were united and secure 'every man under his vine and under his fig tree' (1 Kings 3-4).

As a consequence of this, Solomon was never far from the Jewish mind, and Jesus was no exception (Matt.12:42). When referring to the beautiful lilies that liberally pepper the Mount of Beatitudes overlooking Galilee's famous lake, he suggested not even 'Solomon in all his glory' could be compared to them (Matt. 6:28,29). Yet according to Nathan's message from God, this glorious kingdom would be everlasting, and upon hearing this enthralling news, as already noted, David was almost overcome: 'Who am I, O Lord God....?....thou art great....for there is none like thee, neither is there any God beside thee, according to all that we have heard with our ears. (2 Sam.7:16-18)'

The question Sheba would have asked at this point, an appropriately intelligent one, was whether David understood the prophecy, and if he did, how he envisaged Israel enduring everlastingly. Did he merely accept Nathan's statement at face value, and in praising God trust him to carry out his purposes, but without having any idea what it all meant?

It seems unlikely. For obvious reasons his understanding would have been limited as it is to everyone, 'eternity' not being a concept the finite mind is capable of grappling with successfully. However, David was not a novice in matters of the spirit, who although he had been a military man was nevertheless 'the anointed of the God of Jacob' (2 Sam.23:1), and as such had been the recipient of other revelations from God apart from this one.

He had been 'raised up on high' (2 Sam.23:1) in more ways than one, from the 'sheepcote' to 'greener' pastures (2 Sam.7:8; Ps.23:2), and from the throne of Israel to the 'mouth' of God (Deut. 8:3). He was therefore more than aware of an eternal kingdom already existing, where 'the Lord is King for ever and ever' (Ps.10: 16). Nor was this kingdom and its Sovereign considered abstractly, but from his youth (1 Sam.16:13) David had rejoiced in a personal relationship with the One he called his Shepherd, and 'MY King, and MY God'; in fact, the 'King of glory' (Pss.5:2; 23:1; 24:7-10).

That glory is great which lies 'above the heavens' (Pss.8:1; 138:5), radiating the essence of his Being (Exod.33:19). It permeates every part of the kingdom over which the King reigns supremely (Ps.66:7), a kingdom whose very existence rests upon the covenantal promises he has made with his subjects (Ps.89:3). His voice is majestic, his Word magnified (Pss.29:4; 138:2); his beauty is holiness, his 'hot displeasure' fearful (Ps.6:1; 1 Chron.16: 29), yet 'marvellous loving kindness' also shines through the mercy of the 'Most High' (Pss.17:7; 21:7). David therefore heard Nathan's remarkable message against a rich tapestry of revealed truth, governing his thoughts about the eternal kingdom to be expected.

To begin with, as it was HIS 'house', so also it would be HIS kingdom that would be 'established for ever' (2 Sam.7:16), the implication being twofold: first, that just as the Messiah (the 'seed of David') was to be identified with humanity, likewise so would his kingdom be. No aloof angelic Being were the elect to look for when the Messiah arrived, but a genuine descendant of David (Ruth 4:18-22; Matt.1:5,6), and equally, no 'undiscovered country' (to quote Shakespeare) was the expected everlasting kingdom but one that would be tangible.

This 'holy nation' (1 Peter 2:9), the 'Israel of God' (Gal.6: 16), would possess the hallmarks of the eternal kingdom of heaven itself; its citizens, the privileged 'above all people' (Deut.7:6) selected from every culture on earth (Rev.7:9) and strata of society (Joel 2:28,29; Acts 2:16-18), liberated from spiritual bondage by the truth of which they will be the custodians (John 8:32; 18:37; 1 Tim. 3:15), myriads of precious 'jewels' in the coffers of grace (Mal.3:17).

In the short term, being stained with the blemishes of this world, these 'holy brethren' (Heb.3:1) will require continual washings in the fountain 'for sin and for uncleanness' (Zech.13:1; 1 John 1:7), but God's purposes for them are assured; this 'house of David', the inheritors of his 'established' and everlasting kingdom (2 Sam.7:16; Matt.25:34), is destined to be perfected and presented triumphantly as 'a glorious church' (Ephes.2:27).

The scene is that of a wedding. Solomon was more than familiar with the colourful scenario, 'the day of his espousals' (Cant.3:11): the excited expectancy, the general rejoicing, the laughter and the smiles. But this 'wedding' is on the grandest of all scales, a banquet of loving fellowship accompanying it (Cant.2:4; Rev.19:9) with both eternity and time witnessing unity on the deepest of levels (John 14:20; 15:5); the Messiah as 'bridegroom', the 'new Israel' as his 'bride' (Ephes.2:13-16; 5:25,26), a gracious covenant (Matt.26:27,28) and saving faith (Hab.2:4; Rom.5:1; Gal. 3:11) the 'ring' that binds the two together.

Heaven has witnessed the exchanging of 'vows ('My beloved is mine, and I am his', Cant.2:16; 6:3), as well as of gifts. The 'Son of David' has received her sins and guilt, taking them upon himself (Is.53) and was hanged on a tree in doing so (Deut. 21:22,23), rejected by man and forsaken by his Father (Ps.22:1; Matt.27:46), that his 'fair ones' might be redeemed (Cant.2:10; Is. 53:3,11). In turn these 'daughters of Jerusalem' (Cant.1:5; 3:11) have been enrobed with the 'fine linen, white and clean' (Rev.19: 14) of his purity (Zech.3:1-5; 2 Cor.5:21). It is a transaction hammered into shape on the 'anvil' of suffering; yet not surprisingly of unequal proportions as it was motivated by free grace, the 'bride' receiving more than she expects, and certainly much more than she deserves (1 John 4:19).

But the glories of the Messiah's kingdom (John 17:24), of which said the angel Gabriel there 'shall be no end' (Luke 1:33), are not capable of a limited manifestation. In fact no corner of eternity or time will escape the reverberation of thanksgiving and praise (Ps.150:6). The Creator, whose love for the Christ (Matt.3: 17; 17:5) was the raison d'etre for his marvellous handywork (Col. 1:16), will ensure the universe will blaze with adoration in the knowledge that the King ('the root and the offspring of David', Rev.22:16) has taken up residence among the myriads of worshipping angels (Heb.1:6) and his rejoicing redeemed (Rev.21:3).

However, these will not be the sole witnesses to the glorification of the 'new Israel' promised by God through Nathan (2 Sam.7:16). A day will dawn when the heavens will be swept aside by the giant hand of God, and every eye will witness the majesty of the Son (Rev.1:7), while those who are 'not of this world' (John 18:16) will be the envy of those who are; 'David' the Good Shepherd (Ezek.34:23) arriving from heaven and calling for his 'sheep' (John 10:11,14). No sound could be louder than the blare of the trumpet on that occasion (Matt.24:31; 1 Thess. 4:16), as at Sinai (Exod.19:16); no fear more acute for the unsaved or shock greater for all, than when without warning (Matt.24:42), swift as a winking eye (1 Cor.15:52) and startling as lightning flashing (Matt.24:27), in the firmament will appear the King glorious in sovereign power and majestic in perfect purity (Mark 13:26), his royal family of the redeemed (Mark 3:35) and hosts of angelic courtiers in attendance (Matt.13:41; Heb.12:22).

With what joy the Church triumphant and the Church militant will be united (1 Thess. 4:17), the 'bride adorned for her husband' (Rev.21:2), the patriarchs with the apostles, the child of the old covenant with the child of the new, believing relatives and believing friends; cultural, linguistic and social boundaries no longer possessing relevance (Rev.7;9). All will be everlastingly one, in Christ (Gal.3:28; Ephes.1:10).

The mightiest of all kingdoms will have arrived (Jude v.14), its capital the 'holy city' of the new Jerusalem (Rev.21:2), 'the city of David' whose exulting citizens will have waited at great length for this the most unique and marvellous of all occasions, 'that blessed hope, and the appearing of the great God' and their Saviour the Christ (Titus 2:13): 'ALLELUIA: SALVATION, AND GLORY, AND HONOUR, AND POWER, UNTO THE LORD OUR GOD....ALLELUIA, FOR THE LORD GOD OMNIPOTENT REIGNETH. (Rev.19:1,6)'

But the universe will resound not only with triumphant rejoicing, tragedy's profound sorrow will also be experienced, because the King of all kings and the Lord of all lords will have arrived with eyes blazing with holiness to 'judge and make war' (Rev.19:12,16,21), seeking heaven's vengeance upon the alienated from the one true God (Col.1:21); Satan's children (John 8:44; Ephes.2:2,3), strangers to the faith of Abraham (Gal.3:7,29) and the covenant of grace (2 Thess.1:8; 2 Peter 2:9). Hence, the 'sword' wielded will be 'sharp' (Rev.19:15), signifying the 'slaying' of unbelievers in God's Word (Ephes.6:17; Heb.4:12). If they contributed anything to religious activity, it was in vainly seeking to justify themselves in the sight of God (Job 4:17; 9:2).

Who then will be able to stand (Rev.6: 14-17), as numerous hearts pound with panic, and knees bow and tongues confess the lordship of the Christ (Phil.2:10,11)? Those whimpering with fear will have spent their lives committed to the Buddha, Mohammed, the Virgin, the Hindu gods or darkened 'deities' of various kinds whether mythological or human; anybody but the Son of God (John

14:6). In a declaration of ultimate authority and chilling condemnation they will hear among the most terrible of all statements, 'Ye shall die in your sins' (John 8:24), because 'I never knew you' (Matt.7:23): 'DEPART FROM ME, YE CURSED, INTO EVERLASTING FIRE, PREPARED FOR THE DEVIL AND HIS ANGELS (Matt.25:41; Jude v.6). The final parting of the ways will have begun, the cursed from the blessed, the sheep from the goats (Matt.25:33-46), and the wheat from the chaff (Ps.1: 4; Luke 3:17). There can be no denying of the teaching - unless the Judge is to be considered mistaken or called a liar (John 5:22) - it is fire, everlasting fire (Mark 9:44-48; Luke 16:19-31); the weeping and the wailing will never cease (Matt.25:30-33). And as for the belief in multi-faith religion, the supposed universal Fatherhood of God and the brotherhood of man, the Christ will trample that too into hell (John 3:7; Rev.1:15), for he and he alone is without equal (John 14:6).

Within sight and sound of heaven's righteous fury, the gates of hell flung wide open to receive the damned (Matt.5:29,30), there could not be a greater joy and relief for those left unscathed than to hear the most comforting of all assurances, and spoken by the highest authority: 'Come, ye blessed of my Father, inherit the kingdom prepared for you from the foundation of the world. (Matt. 25:34)' To hear such words should surely be the aim of every human creature; not to hear them the ultimate failure.

The fourfold statement is brief, and understandable the joyous thanksgiving (and humble surprise) upon hearing it; that one's soul has everlastingly (Jer.31:3) been the object of the divine love (Mal.1:2; Rom.9:13), one's name unique in the annals of heaven and written in the book of life with blood most precious (Rev.20:12-15).

Could there be a warmer and more loving welcome ('Come'), a more authoritative reason for responding ('ye blessed of my Father'), a more profound stimulus for eternal adoration ('inherit the kingdom'), and a greater hint of the glory awaiting the elect ('PREPARED for YOU from the foundation of the world')? And yet what will have been spoken is as if peering through the keyhole, the door still having to be opened for the eye to witness the fullness of the splendour, the ear the beauty of the sounds that permeate heaven, or the soul to be ravished by the spiritual richness of it all (Is.64:4; 1 Cor.2:9).

BRIGHTER THAN THE SUN

Sheba must have been entranced. Having plied her host with numerous questions, at last she had reached the climax of her quest. She had learned a great deal about the Messiah, and now she had been led to his eternal throne, the throne of 'David' (2 Sam.7: 16). Had Solomon's father not been promised that 'the fruit' of his body would sit upon it (Ps.132:11)?

Central to everything existing both in heaven and upon the earth (Matt.11:25), from this immovable throne were issued immutable commands (Rev.4:2) by an irresistible Sovereign. Like lightning rebellious Lucifer fell (Is.14:12-14; Luke 10:18), and as swiftly light arose upon a vast and blackened space, followed by creation's intricacies slotting neatly into place (Job 38-41). Man included, woman too, living souls who disobeyed the One who formed them and entered 'death' at his command (Gen.1-3; Rom.7: 24; 1 Cor.15:22).

Mighty empires may straddle the globe, yet will crumble; conquering kingdoms will come, and go; arrogant autocrats will arrive, but depart (Is.40:21-31; Rom.9:17). Time will have swept them aside, but the Majesty on high (Heb.1:3; 12:2) will have decided the precise moment of their appearance as well as that of their demise (Ps.31:15; Prov.20:24). He is the Holy One, the Word of life (1 John 1:1), the Creator of all things and for whom all things were created (Is.40:28; John 1:3; Col.1:16), upholding everything by an authoritative command (Gen.1:1; John 1:1).

And at the throne all questions are solved, every answer discovered, for the Victor has a giant book in his possession. It is perfectly sealed, only he can read its contents, unlock the secrets, reveal its mysteries: the mind and the heart of God (John 1:1-14), his incomparable and immutable decrees affecting every aspect of world history (his-story), all the avenues of intellectual study and debate, and each individual born of Adam (Rev.5:1-7). No one asks questions at the throne on high, there is no need, because 'the treasures of wisdom and knowledge' are no longer hidden but are on permanent display (Col.2:3).

To Solomon was revealed the fact that a throne is 'established by righteousness' (Prov.16:12; 25:5), how much more therefore would this be so of the throne upon which is eternally seated the One who possesses 'the sceptre of righteousness' (Pss.11:7; 45:6; Heb.1:8).

Described 'as the sun' (Ps.89:36), it generates both heat and light,the symbols of perfect holiness and ultimate truth (Pss.47:8; 96: 13). Here reality is confronted, no façade can be presented; no lie exist. Reflected in the radiant glare of God's face, described as possessing the clarity of crystal (Rev.4:3; 21:11), only that which has the transparency of perfect purity is welcome (1 Cor.3:11-14). The King, like any king over whom he rules, 'scattereth away all evil with his eyes' (Prov. 20:8).

Sheba must have suffered yet another shock upon learning this, truth so far removed from her cultural background, and surely she asked the question on many a lip since that time: who, then, can stand before such glory (Ps.76:7; Rev.6:17)? Then she would have remembered what she had been taught: the necessity and efficacy of atoning blood (Lev.17:11), the sufficiency and efficiency of divine intercession (Exod.28:38; Numb.6:24-26), as well as the gracious provision of acceptance ('at-one-ment') before almighty God. After all, although the throne of 'David' was prepared for judgment (Ps.9:7), goodness being an integral part of his character (Exod.33:19), it is also upheld by mercy (Prov.20:28).

For this reason it is enveloped, not in gloom, but in adoration and praise as myriads of angels (Matt.26:53) give vent to the triumph and glory (Ps.103:21) of the Messiah with which the magnificent court of heaven is unceasingly filled (John 17:4,24). These flames of holy fire (Ps.104:4; Heb.1:7), rising and descending over the throne (Gen.28:12; John 1:51), fly through the candescence of worship at its most elevated: 'Praise ye THE LORD from the heavens: praise him in the heights. Praise ye him, all his angels, praise ye him, all his hosts. (Ps.148:1,2). The music of heaven is the most beautiful of all sounds, surpassing anything that can be heard on earth (Is.64:4; 1 Cor.2:9).

Vast though these angelic armies are (Heb.1:6), their limitations are known to the royal court (Job 4:18). They are ever aware of the radiance of the divine face, reflecting an aspect of it in their own (Acts 6:15), but are not permitted to see it (Is.6:2). They overshadow the throne, but cannot sit upon it; they possess feet, but humbly cover them lest they be tempted to stand and linger before the One to whom they minister (Heb.1:14). They know of his love (1 John 4:8), but instead cry, 'Holy, holy, holy' (Is.6:2,3). Obeisance is their duty, reverential awe their delight. But the angelic hosts are not alone in their joyfulness. A vast multitude, which the triune God alone is capable of counting, adds its rejoicing in triumphant melody. The royal court has not heard this song before; it is the 'new song' of redemption, not the old song of creation (Rev.4:11; 5:9), for the innumerable company (Rev.7:9), assembled before the thrice-holy Potentate seated in majesty (1 Tim.6:15), have the most to exult in and sing about.

These are much more than the privileged citizens of 'David's' kingdom; they are members of the royal family. Their eyes do not require covering, because they bear the family likeness (1 John 3:2), nor do they need to cover their feet (Is.6:2), for to be seated on the throne of grace (Rev.3:21), or to stand before it (Rev. 7:9), are positions expected of them. Those who belong to the family of the King-Priest (Mark 3:33-35; Zech.6:12,13), who being a kingdom of priests have continual access to the Almighty (Rev.1: 6) are not only joyful observers of 'David's' glory (Ezek.34:23; John 17:24), but also rejoicing sharers in it (Rom.8:30).

And how impossible it is to describe what the redeemed are everlastingly observing at the throne (Col.3:4). If eye and ear are strangers to it, then the tongue certainly is (Is.64:4; 1 Cor.2:9), as is the hand that writes the prose. But to know the soul is swept sinless (1 John 1:7), and righteous (2 Cor.5:21), beyond the reach of vexation (2 Peter 2:8), the taint of uncertainties and the restraints imposed upon it by time, is surely to grasp the hem of understanding.

Equally, to be assured of eternal 'rest' (Heb.4:11), and enraptured with joyous adoration ('SALVATION TO OUR GOD WHICH SITTETH UPON THE THRONE, AND UNTO THE LAMB', Rev.7:10), is to have entered albeit partially into the experience. It is to have arrived at the most exquisite of all locations, the venue where unfathomable grace and absolute truth (John 1:14) meet in that 'name which is above every name' (Phil.2: 9), the name that brought Sheba over a thousand miles in her quest (1 Kings 10:1-3).

What a plethora of paradoxes are to be discovered at the throne: the Son of God becoming the Son of man (Mark 2:10), the eternal Word made temporal flesh (John 1:14), the substitution of heaven's wealth with earth's poverty (2 Cor.8:9), and the sinner's Saviour 'made sin' (2 Cor.5:21). Likewise, the Judge of mankind being judged by man (John 5:22); the High Priest 'for ever' by the high priest for time (Matt.26:62; Heb.6:20). Then, the Creator of all things dying upon a cross whose wood he had made (Col.1:16), crucified by men he had created (Gen.1:26), and on a hill designated by him for the task (Ps.2:6). And what about Judah's Lion and God's slain Lamb (Rev.5: 5,6), the Carpenter's donkey (Matt.21:7) and the King's horse (Rev.19:11); the 'sceptre' of reed (Matt.27:29) and the rod of iron (Rev.19:15), the blood-spattered robe (John 19:1) and the robe of blood (Rev.19:13), the crown of thorns (John 19:5) and the Crown of crowns (Rev.19:12)?

Thus what grace has caused the exultation, and how many are the reasons for it! To begin with, how amazed the redeemed are at being present, safe and secure among the family of God's covenant people, enclosed not within the fist of retribution but upon the palm of his sensitive hand (John 10:28); gathered as sheep (Matt.25:32) in the good Shepherd's fold (Ezek.34:23), garnered as wheat in the 'barn' of redemption (Ps.1: 4; Matt.3:12; 13:30). And what a cross section of humanity surrounds them, bound together by 'one faith, one Lord, one baptism' (Ephes. 4:4,5), a unity the world has yearned after since its fall but could not achieve (John 17:21).

From history's beginning, when redemption's story was first related (Gen.3:15,21), through numerous generations and from all points of the compass (Matt.8:11; Rev.7:9), they had been beckoned by the Father and drawn (John 6:44,45,65) by the Spirit to embrace the Son (Ps.2:12; Heb.6:18,19), either in anticipation of his arrival upon earth or as a result of it (Rom.3:25). The mighty and the minute in the faith, the sages and the simpletons, the men and the women, the boys and the girls: the elect, chosen not en masse but individually and with loving care (Matt.10:30), each name known to the triune God before the dawning of the universe's first day and as already mentioned, carefully registered in the ledger of life (Dan.7:9,10; Rev.20:12-15).

There, amidst the acclamation before the eternal throne these 'vessels of mercy' (Rom.9:23) possess the answers to two questions that puzzled them in time: why has God everlastingly loved and chosen them, and does he love one of his children more than another? How seemingly obtuse is the first answer, how apparently irrational, but 'love divine, all loves excelling' flies higher than the heavens and refuses to succumb to the measurements of man (Is.55:9); no reason, or excuse, is given to express its affection.

At one time unattractive to him, unworthy of him, unloving towards him, the elect cry out 'Why us, Lord, why?' (1 John 4:10,19), and sovereign Love replies, 'Why not? (Rom.9:16)' There is no answer to that, just surrender to astonishing grace, as Jacob and Esau discovered (Mal.1:2,3; Rom. 9:13). The former was as wretched as the latter (Gen.25:31-34); the marvel though is not that God loves one and not another, but because of mankind's alienation from him as a result of the fall (Col.1:21), that he loves anyone.

But how immense is the congregation, and with what distinction did great numbers in it serve their Lord during their lives upon the earth; what great heights were reached, what mighty endeavours were achieved! Warriors for him in prayerful word and courageous deed, and now before the throne in company with their lowly brethren and sisters! How much greater must be his love, much warmer his smile, for the achievers than for the simple believers!

Even if reassurance is necessary, the appearance at the throne reveals this is not so, salvation being of grace not deeds (Ephes.2:8). The Son's 'deep, deep love' is spread widely and equally over his entire family (Matt.20:12-16) and each separate individual (Mark 3:33-35), a reflection of the love eternally existing within the blessed Trinity (Prov.8:30; John 17:24) and now realised within the perfected community of saints: love at its deepest, for God (Deut. 6:5) and for each other (Matt.22:37-39).

Heaven's gates were flung wide open for all of them (Heb.4: 9), but no one can stand taller than another in his own eyes when passing through to glory (Ephes.3:8), where all who do so tread softly, aware that the righteous are 'scarcely saved' (1 Peter 4:18). In any case, are they not all just 'babes' in the sight of their Lord (Matt. 11:25)? In fact, heaven resounds to the pre-eminence of the Redeemer, and he alone, where 'greatness' and 'achievement' have met at their most sublime. All else pales into insignificance, even irrelevance: 'THINE is the kingdom, and the power, and the glory' – and FOR EVER (Matt.6:13).

The music of adoration soars towards a crescendo, as in its fullness is experienced his immeasurable love for each of the assembled redeemed (Ephes. 3:17-19), an everlasting passion incapable of diminishing in its intensity (Jer.31:3). And for the love of that soul, lost within fallen mankind and under God's curse (Gen.2:17; 1 Cor.15:22) and Satan's dominion (Col.1:13), he passed through the ranks of worshipping angels (Heb.1:5) and entered the world to search, to find and to rescue. The rest is glorious history: through the proclamation of the 'good tidings', the world's 'ashes', mourning and heaviness were exchanged for heaven's beauty, joy and praise (Is.61:1-3).

But the apex of this marvellous splendour is to 'see him as he is' (1 John 3:2), even to behold his face (1 Cor.13:12). It is the ultimate reality: the triumphant climax of all he has achieved for his people, and the fruition of the faith he has gifted them with (Ephes.2:8). The word to Moses was adamant, 'Thou canst NOT see my face: for there shall no man see me, and live', God insisting, 'my face shall NOT be seen' (Exod.33:20-23). What Moses saw was extremely limited, but even so, afterwards such was the radiance of his face he was obliged to cover it when speaking to the nation (Exod.34:33-35). One is left to imagine how glorious must be the countenance of the one who looks eternally into the face of God.

Now though Moses, together with all assembled at the throne, are singing the 'national anthem' of rejoicing praise even as they gaze into the Lord's penetrating and holy eyes of flame (Rev.19:12), because they are 'like him' (1 John 3:2), perfected in him and sharing his radiance. '...THOU WAST SLAIN', they exult triumphantly, 'AND HAST REDEEMED US TO GOD BY THY BLOOD OUT OF EVERY KINDRED, AND TONGUE, AND

PEOPLE, AND NATION' (Rev.5:9). Upon earth, with a quiet excitement, the redeemed anticipate joining that great throng of worshippers. Who will not desire to be numbered among them?

APPENDIX

It was time for Sheba to make the long journey home again. She had asked her profound questions, and had evidently received satisfactory answers, because she bade farewell to her host on a very optimistic note: **'Blessed be the Lord thy God, which delighted in thee to set thee on the throne of Israel, because the Lord loved Israel FOR EVER...'** (1 Kings 10:9).

Her quest had concerned 'the name of the Lord' (1 Kings 10:1) and although she returned home with a limited understanding of the subject – 'God having provided some better thing' for future generations (Heb.11:40) - nevertheless she had learned many things about what today is called the Gospel, and not least the secret revealed to David which his son Solomon possessed. As Joshua led the old Israel into the promised land (Josh.3), so 'Joshua' (Jesus) leads the new Israel (the Christian Church) into the land of greatest promise (Heb.4:1-11). Sheba's quest had ended.